T0006397

THE COMPLETE INSTANT POT COOKBOOK

Innovative Recipes to Slow Cook, Air Fry, and Pressure Cook

CONTENTS

ONE APPLIANCE, NINE FUNCTIONS

A multicooker appliance that can be used across a broad range of cooking applications, and combines many kitchen appliances into the one space-saving machine, is every cook's dream. While a multicooker won't shop for you or chop your ingredients, it will streamline the cooking process for a variety of cooking functions. Less hands-on cooking and less washing-up throughout the cooking process are the rewards when using a multicooker. All this time saved means that you'll be getting delicious meals on the table a lot more quickly.

There is an assortment of Instant Pot models for sale in the marketplace. For this book, we used the 8-liter Instant Pot Duo Crisp + Air Fryer when testing our recipes. Before using your Instant Pot, read the safety and operating instructions for your specific model.

GENERAL SAFETY

Carefully read your appliance's operating manual. Failure to adhere to the safety instructions may result in serious injury. Take care with children and pets around your appliance, and treat it as you would an oven or stovetop.

To avoid electric shock, it is important that you are aware that the base of the appliance and the air-fryer lid contain electrical components that should not come into contact with water or other liquids; they should be wiped down rather than rinsed.

The appliance should not be placed directly on a heat source.

Pressure-cooking safety Before using this function, consult your appliance's manual for all safety checks required. Never use this mode without the inner pot containing liquid. Ensure that the correct lid is used, the lid is locked, and valves are correctly positioned.

Never open or move the appliance while the quick-release valve is up; wait until the pressure has completely dropped.

Do not fill the appliance's inner pot more than two-thirds full (as indicated on the pot), and no more than half full of food that will expand during cooking, such as rice or pasta.

Take care to protect yourself when releasing the pressure. Do not touch the quick-release valve directly with your hands; instead, use the end of a wooden spoon.

To avoid scalding, ensure that your face and body are positioned away from the appliance when steam is released either naturally or with the quick-release method, and when removing the lid.

Air-fryer cooking safety When using the air-fryer function, ensure that there is sufficient air flow around the base of the appliance, and do not obstruct the vents of the air-fryer lid. Do not overfill the air-fryer basket.

CLEANING

Cool the appliance before cleaning and follow the manufacturer's instructions, for safety and to preserve the life of your appliance.

SAUTÉ Use this function with the inner pot and without a lid to sauté, sear, stir-fry, and reduce, same as you would in a pan. Select the low or high setting, and once the temperature is reached, the appliance will register "hot."

DEHYDRATE This function uses the principles of the air fryer to create fast circulating air but at much lower temperatures, so foods dehydrate over a long cooking time. Ingredients can be placed in the air-fryer basket, using either the steamer rack with handles or the perforated tray, and sealed with the air-fryer lid. We recommend purchasing a 5-tier dehydrator rack to get the best use of available space.

RICE The model we used did not have a rice preset for rice, but you can still cook rice using the pressure-cooker function and lid. On average, use a 1:1 cup water to rice ratio, for white or brown rice.

AIR FRY Use this function to circulate air around food for a crisp result using less oil. Depending on the recipe, use either the inner pot or air-fryer basket with the air-fryer lid. The appliance will display "turn food" halfway through cooking. After turning, cooking will resume once the lid is replaced.

STEAM This functions in the same way as **PRESSURE COOK**, as it steams under pressure. Use this mode with the inner pot, steam rack with handles, and pressure-cooker lid for vegetables, chicken, and fish, ensuring at least 1 cup (250ml) of liquid is in the inner pot. Use the quick-release method to depressurize. Once time is reached, the appliance automatically defaults to "keep warm."

ROAST This function is the same as **AIR FRY**, with a prompt to turn food halfway through cooking. Use either the air-fryer basket, inner pot, or ovenproof cookware in the inner pot, with the air-fryer lid.

SLOW COOK Use this function to transform tough cheap cuts of meat into delicious melt-in-the-mouth dinners. Use with the inner pot and pressure-cooker lid. The temperature displays as either low or high. Once the cooking time is reached, the appliance automatically defaults to "keep warm."

PRESSURE COOK This function uses steam pressure to raise the boiling point of water for fast cooking. The inner pot and pressure-cooker lid are required. The position of the quick-release valve indicates pressure level. The appliance is pressurized once the valve has popped above lid level and depressurized when it has fallen. This function has three stages: coming up to pressure, cooking, and depressurization. During depressurization food continues to cook. There are two ways to steam release: natural release and quick release. When the quick-release button has popped up, the appliance will steadily release steam over time. To quick-release steam, the valve must be turned manually.

BAKE This function is similar to **AIR FRY**. Either use the air-fryer basket or place a cake pan on the steam rack in the inner pot, with the air-fryer lid. The temperature can be manually adjusted, so you can bake everything from casseroles to cakes and other baked goods. For even cooking, allow 1in (2.5cm) space around the cookware.

GET A HANDLE ON YOUR INSTANT POT

APPLIANCE PARTS

01 Air-fryer lid
Use with **AIR FRY**, **ROAST**, **BAKE**, and **DEHYDRATE** cooking functions.

02 Cooker base + control panel
The cooker base must always be used with the inner pot or the air-fryer basket and accessories. The control panel shows: time, temperature, and pressure display for the different cooking functions.

03 Steam rack with handles
A multifunctional rack that allows for air flow and stacking, with handles to assist with removal.

04 Perforated tray
Also known as dehydrating/broiling tray, it fits in the air-fryer basket, creating another level on which to stack food.

05 Pressure-cooker lid
Use with **PRESSURE COOK** and **SLOW COOK** functions only.

06 Air-fryer basket
Use with **AIR FRY**, **BAKE**, and **DEHYDRATE** cooking functions.

07 Inner pot
Use the inner pot to **SAUTÉ**, cook rice, **SLOW COOK**, **STEAM**, **PRESSURE COOK**, and **BAKE**. The pot is hot to touch. For handling and removing, wear gloves or heat protection to protect your hands. Also, take care to wear long-sleeved clothing to avoid burns when reaching into the inner pot. The pot includes fill lines for safe volume levels.

CONTROL PANEL BASICS

ON Appliance is in preheat mode.

OFF Appliance is in standby mode.

LID Alert if incorrect lid is used or is not secured, or due to no lid in place.

TIME When program is in use, counts down cooking time. Time is also displayed when "delay start" is selected and until the program begins, and displays with functions that default to "keep warm," showing how long food has been warming.

HOT When using **SAUTÉ** mode and temperature is reached.

END Program is completed and does not revert to "keep warm."

FOOD BURN This warning can appear when food is overheating and/or when there is not enough liquid. Consult your appliance's manual for specific guidance.

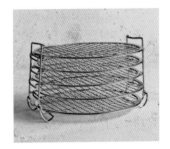

A 5-tier dehydrator rack allows you to make the most of space in the appliance, so you can dry more fruits, vegetables, and meats to lock in nutrition.

SAUTÉ

Ditch the frying pan and use your Instant Pot instead. Use the sauté function on your multicooker to sear to perfection and bring stir-fries, noodles, and quick-to-assemble meals to the table with ease.

BROWN SAUCE PORK NOODLES

Prep 10 mins   **Sauté** 13 mins   **Serves** 4   Dairy-free

1 tbsp peanut or vegetable oil
3 garlic cloves, crushed
3 tsp finely grated fresh ginger
6 spring onions (scallions),
   thinly sliced
1½ lb (750g) ground pork (see tips)
½ cup (140g) ground bean sauce
   (see tips)
¼ cup (70g) oyster sauce (see tips)
½ cup (125ml) chicken stock
   (see tips)
14oz (400g) shelf-stable (wok-ready)
   fresh udon noodles
8oz (225g) bok choy, quartered
   lengthwise
to serve: Asian fried shallots,
   extra sliced spring onion (scallion),
   and chili oil

1 Select **SAUTÉ** high heat. Add oil to the inner pot. When the inner pot is hot, add garlic, ginger, and spring onions; sauté, stirring, for 1 minute or until softened. Add ground pork and sauté for a further 8 minutes, breaking up pork with a wooden spoon, until cooked through.

2 Add combined sauces and chicken stock to the inner pot; stir until well combined. Add noodles and bok choy; sauté for 4 minutes until noodles are heated through and bok choy is wilted.

3 Serve noodle mixture topped with Asian fried shallots and extra spring onion, drizzled with a little chili oil.

TIPS To make this dish vegetarian, use plant-based mince, a vegetarian stir-fry sauce in place of oyster sauce, and vegetable stock instead of chicken.

Chinese ground bean sauce, made with fermented yellow soybeans, is available from Asian grocers and supermarkets.

11

GOCHUJANG BEEF & VEGGIE STIR-FRY

Prep 10 mins   **Sauté** 35 mins   **Serves** 4   Dairy-free

¼ cup (65g) gochujang (Korean chili paste) (see tip)
2 tbsp soy sauce
2 tbsp rice vinegar
1 tbsp honey
2 x 8oz (225g) sirloin steaks
1 tbsp sesame oil
2 bunches broccolini, about 13½oz (380g) in total, thick stems halved lengthwise
8oz (225g) sugar snap peas
1 tsp finely grated fresh ginger
1 garlic clove, crushed
½ lb (200g) Napa or Savoy cabbage, coarsely shredded
½ cup (120g) kimchi
¼ cup (35g) salted roasted peanuts, coarsely chopped
to serve: shelf-stable (wok-ready) fresh ramen noodles (use unflavored medium noodles)

1 Combine gochujang, soy sauce, rice vinegar, and honey in a small bowl. Combine steaks with ¼ cup (60ml) of the sauce mixture and set aside.

2 Select **SAUTÉ** high heat and preheat for 5 minutes. When the inner pot is hot, add steaks and **SAUTÉ** for 5 minutes on each side until browned and medium-rare (cooking time will vary depending on the thickness of the steaks). Transfer steaks to a plate, cover, and allow to rest for 8 minutes. Wipe the bottom of the inner pot with paper towel.

3 Add half of the sesame oil to the inner pot, then add broccolini; **SAUTÉ** for 2 minutes. Add sugar snap peas and **SAUTÉ** for a further 3 minutes or until vegetables are tender and bright green. Transfer vegetables to a plate and cover to keep warm.

4 Add remaining sesame oil to the inner pot, then add ginger, garlic, Napa cabbage, and kimchi; **SAUTÉ**, stirring frequently, for 4 minutes or until Napa cabbage is slightly wilted. Return broccolini and sugar snap peas to the inner pot with remaining sauce mixture; toss until well combined.

5 Cut steaks into thin slices. Heat noodles according to the package directions and serve with stir-fried vegetables and steak, scattered with peanuts.

TIP Gochujang is a spicy Korean red chili paste available from larger supermarkets and Asian grocers.

SHRIMP SAN CHOY BAU

Prep 20 mins   **Sauté** 7 mins   **Makes** 16   Dairy-free   Pescatarian

1 tbsp peanut or vegetable oil
3 garlic cloves, crushed
3 tsp finely grated fresh ginger
6 spring onions (scallions),
  thinly sliced
1½lb (750g) shrimp, peeled,
  deveined, butterflied
8oz (227g) can sliced water
  chestnuts, drained, coarsely
  chopped
4oz (120g) snow peas, sliced
1 tbsp coconut aminos
1 tbsp brown sugar
2 tbsp oyster sauce
1 tsp sesame oil
1 tbsp lime juice
⅓ cup (20g) chopped cilantro
  stems and leaves
16 leaves from 2 hearts of
  Romaine lettuce
to serve: bean sprouts, fried
  noodles, and roasted peanuts

1 Select **SAUTÉ** high heat. Add oil to the inner pot. When the inner pot is hot, add garlic, ginger, and spring onions; **SAUTÉ**, stirring, for 1 minute until softened. Add shrimp and **SAUTÉ**, stirring, for a further 4 minutes or until almost cooked through.
2 Add water chestnuts, snow peas, coconut aminos, brown sugar, oyster sauce, sesame oil, and lime juice to the inner pot; **SAUTÉ**, stirring, for 2 minutes or until sauce is slightly reduced and shrimp are coated. Stir through half of the cilantro.

3 To serve, divide san choy bau mixture among lettuce leaves; top with bean sprouts, fried noodles, peanuts, and remaining cilantro.

TIP You can use 2 tablespoons of kecap manis (Indonesian sweet soy sauce) instead of the coconut aminos and brown sugar.

TARRAGON CHICKEN & GNOCCHI POT PIE

Prep 5 mins   **Sauté** 25 mins   **Air Fry** 10 mins   **Serves** 4   Gluten-free   Good to freeze

¼ cup (60ml) extra virgin olive oil
2¼lb (1kg) boneless, skinless chicken thighs, cut into 1in (2.5cm) pieces
2 tbsp (30g) butter
3 shallots, about 2½oz (75g) in total, thinly sliced
2 garlic cloves, finely chopped
½ cup (125ml) dry white wine
1½ tbsp Dijon mustard
¾ cup (180ml) gluten-free chicken stock
⅔ cup (160ml) heavy cream
1 tbsp finely chopped tarragon
16oz (450g) package gluten-free gnocchi
to serve: extra chopped tarragon

1 Select **SAUTÉ** high heat and preheat for 5 minutes.
2 Season the chicken with salt and pepper. When the inner pot is hot, add 1 tablespoon of the oil and half of the chicken; **SAUTÉ** for 5 minutes or until browned. Transfer chicken to a plate. Repeat with another 1 tablespoon of the oil and remaining chicken; transfer to plate.
3 Add butter, shallots, and garlic to the inner pot; **SAUTÉ**, stirring, for 3 minutes or until shallots are softened. Add wine and sauté for a further 2 minutes or until reduced. Add mustard, stock, cream, and tarragon; stir to combine. Bring to a simmer. Return chicken to the inner pot and **SAUTÉ** for 10 minutes or until chicken is just cooked through.

Turn off **SAUTÉ**. Transfer mixture to an 8in (20cm) pie dish, ensuring the dish fits in the inner pot. Rinse the inner pot and return to the appliance.
4 Combine gnocchi and remaining oil in a medium bowl; season with salt and pepper. Scatter gnocchi evenly over the chicken mixture. Place pie dish in the inner pot. Cover with the air-fryer lid. Select **AIR FRY** and set temperature to 400°F/200°C and time for 10 minutes; **AIR FRY**, turning halfway through cooking, until gnocchi is golden.
5 Serve scattered with extra chopped tarragon.

TIP If the top of the "pie" looks a little dry, spray or brush with extra oil both halfway through and at the end of cooking.

MIDDLE EASTERN SPICED LAMB (LAHMACUN)

Prep 10 mins   **Air Fry** 8 mins   **Sauté** 16 mins   **Serves** 4   Dairy-free   Good to freeze

4 x 6in (15cm) round pita breads, about 14oz (400g) in total

1 tbsp extra virgin olive oil

1 medium red onion, about 6oz (170g), finely chopped

2 garlic cloves, crushed

1lb (500g) ground lamb

2 tsp sumac

1 tbsp baharat (see tip)

8oz (225g) cherry roma tomatoes, halved

15.5oz (439g) can chickpeas, drained, rinsed

2 tbsp finely chopped mint leaves

2 tbsp pomegranate molasses

⅔ cup (180g) hummus

⅓ cup (50g) pine nuts, toasted

to serve: extra pomegranate molasses and extra mint leaves

1 Insert the air-fryer basket with the basket base into the inner pot. Arrange pita breads standing upright around the side of the air-fryer basket. Cover with the air-fryer lid. Select **AIR FRY**, set temperature to 400°F/200°C and time for 8 minutes; **AIR FRY** until pita breads are crisp. Taking care, remove the air-fryer basket with pita breads and set aside.

2 Select **SAUTÉ** high heat. Add oil to the inner pot. When the inner pot is hot, add onion and **SAUTÉ**, stirring, for 3 minutes until softened. Add garlic and lamb; **SAUTÉ** for a further 8 minutes, breaking up the ground lamb with a wooden spoon, until cooked through. Add spices, baby plum tomatoes, chickpeas, the 2 tablespoons finely chopped mint, and the molasses; **SAUTÉ** for 5 minutes. Season with salt and freshly ground black pepper to taste.

3 Spread each pita bread with 2 tablespoons of the hummus and top with lamb mixture; drizzle with extra pomegranate molasses, and scatter with pine nuts and extra mint leaves to serve.

TIP An all-purpose spice mix widely used in Middle Eastern cuisines, baharat can be found at specialty grocers and larger supermarkets.

ONE-POT PAPPARDELLE BOLOGNESE

Prep 10 mins   **Sauté** 35 mins   **Serves** 4   Good to freeze

1½ oz (50g) piece of pancetta
1 medium onion, about 5½oz (150g)
1 medium carrot, about 5oz (140g)
1 celery stalk
1½ tbsp extra virgin olive oil
1lb (500g) mixed ground pork
    and veal
6oz (170g) can tomato purée
½ cup (125ml) red wine
3 cups (750ml) chicken stock
sprig of rosemary
1lb (500g) fresh pappardelle
1 cup (250ml) boiling water
to serve: finely grated Parmesan
    cheese

1 Finely chop the pancetta, onion, carrot, and celery.

2 Select **SAUTÉ** high heat. Add oil to the inner pot. When the inner pot is hot, add pancetta and ground meats; **SAUTÉ** for 8 minutes, stirring frequently, breaking up pork and veal with a wooden spoon, until browned. Add chopped vegetables and **SAUTÉ** for a further 4 minutes, stirring occasionally, until softened. Add tomato purée and **SAUTÉ** for 3 minutes or until the color deepens. Add wine and **SAUTÉ** for a further 5 minutes until almost completely reduced. Add chicken stock and rosemary; **SAUTÉ** until mixture boils, then cook for a further 10 minutes until slightly reduced.

3 Add pappardelle to the inner pot; pour over the 1 cup (250ml) boiling water. Cover pot with aluminum foil and sauté for 5 minutes or until pasta is tender.

4 Serve pappardelle bolognese sprinkled with grated Parmesan cheese.

STICKY POMEGRANATE SALMON WITH EGGPLANT

Prep 20 mins   **Sauté** 16 mins   **Serves** 4   Gluten-free   Pescatarian

½ cup (125ml) olive oil
1 large eggplant, about 1lb 7oz
(650g), cut into 1in (2.5cm) cubes
1 medium red onion, about 6oz
(170g), cut into thin wedges
2 garlic cloves, crushed
2 tbsp ras el hanout (Moroccan
spice mix)
1 tsp ground cumin
1 tsp ground coriander
4 x 8oz (225g) middle-cut salmon
fillets, skinned, cut into 1in
(2.5cm) cubes
¼ cup (60ml) pomegranate
molasses
½ cup (140g) Greek-style yogurt
1 tbsp tahini
1 tbsp lemon juice
¼ cup (5g) small flat-leaf
parsley leaves
3 cups (60g) arugula
to serve: extra pomegranate
molasses

1 Select **SAUTÉ** high heat. Add ⅓ cup (80ml) of the oil to the inner pot. When the inner pot is hot, add eggplant and **SAUTÉ**, stirring, for 6 minutes or until golden and softened. Add onion and garlic; **SAUTÉ**, stirring, for a further 4 minutes until softened. Add ras el hanout, cumin, and coriander; sauté for 30 seconds. Transfer vegetables to a plate and cover to keep warm.

2 Add remaining oil to the inner pot. When oil is hot, add salmon and **SAUTÉ** for 4 minutes, turning gently, until golden. Stir through 2 tablespoons of the pomegranate molasses and **SAUTÉ** for 1 minute or until caramelized. Season with salt and freshly ground black pepper to taste.

3 In a small bowl, combine remaining pomegranate molasses with yogurt, tahini, and lemon juice.

4 Toss eggplant mixture, parsley, and arugula together; top with salmon and drizzle with extra pomegranate molasses. Serve with tahini yogurt.

CHICKEN SCALOPPINE WITH MUSHROOMS & SPINACH

Prep 10 mins   **Air Fry** 13 mins   **Sauté** 12 mins   **Serves** 4

1lb (500g) premade gnocchi
⅓ cup (80ml) olive oil
2 tbsp rosemary leaves
¼ cup (20g) finely grated Parmesan cheese
2lb (800g) boneless, skinless chicken breasts, cut in half horizontally
3 tsp coarsely chopped thyme leaves
⅔ lb (350g) mixed mushrooms (see tip), thickly sliced
3 tbsp (40g) butter, chopped
1 tbsp lemon juice
1 garlic clove, crushed
½ cup (15g) coarsely chopped flat-leaf parsley
3 cups (100g) baby spinach leaves

1 Place gnocchi in a bowl and season with salt and pepper. Add 1 tablespoon of the oil, the rosemary, and Parmesan cheese; toss well to combine.
2 Place the air-fryer basket with the basket base in the inner pot. Add gnocchi mixture to the air-fryer basket. Cover with the air-fryer lid. Select **AIR FRY**, set temperature to 400°F/200°C, and time for 13 minutes; **AIR FRY** until gnocchi is warmed and crisp. Taking care, remove the air-fryer basket with gnocchi; cover, and set aside to keep warm.
3 Scatter chicken with thyme and season with salt and pepper. Select **SAUTÉ** high heat. Add 1½ tablespoons of the oil to the inner pot. When the inner pot is hot, add chicken and **SAUTÉ** in two batches for 2 minutes on each side, or until golden and cooked through. Transfer chicken to a plate and cover to keep warm.
4 Add remaining oil to the inner pot, add mushrooms and season with salt and pepper; **SAUTÉ**, stirring for 4 minutes until golden. Turn off the appliance. Add butter, lemon juice, garlic, parsley, and spinach to the inner pot; stir until butter has melted and spinach is slightly wilted.
5 Serve chicken scaloppine with mushroom mixture and gnocchi.

TIP We used a mixture of trumpet, shimeji, oyster, portobello (cremini), and shiitake mushrooms.

RICE

Your Instant Pot makes cooking rice a breeze. Whether it's risotto or jollof rice, claypot chicken or shrimp bibimbap, you can be sure of perfectly cooked rice every time.

RATATOUILLE RICE

Prep 10 mins   **Sauté** 12 mins   **Pressure Cook** 4 mins   **Serves** 4   Gluten-free   Vegetarian

⅓ cup (80ml) olive oil
1 medium eggplant, about 10oz
   (300g), cut into 1in (2.5cm) pieces
1 medium red onion, about 6oz
   (180g), cut into thin wedges
5oz (175g) sweet mini red peppers,
   halved, seeds removed
2 small zucchini, about 6oz (180g) in
   total, cut into 1in (2.5cm) pieces
4 garlic cloves, crushed
½ cup (15g) basil leaves, torn
1½ cups (300g) long-grain rice
12oz (375g) can cherry tomatoes
2 cups (500ml) vegetable stock
to serve: goat cheese and extra
   basil leaves

1 Select **SAUTÉ** high heat. Add ¼ cup (60ml) of the oil to the inner pot. When the inner pot is hot, add eggplant and **SAUTÉ**, stirring, for 6 minutes or until golden and softened. Transfer eggplant to a plate and cover to keep warm until needed.
2 Add remaining oil to the inner pot, then add onion, peppers, and zucchini; **SAUTÉ**, stirring, for 4 minutes until browned. Add garlic, basil, and rice; stir to coat the rice. Turn off **SAUTÉ**. Stir tomatoes, stock, and eggplant into the inner pot. Transfer mixture to a deep 9in (23cm) round cake pan or other pan that fits inside the appliance.

3 Clean the inner pot and return to the appliance. Add 1 cup (250ml) water to the pot. Place the wire rack in the inner pot, then place the pan on top. Cover with the pressure-cooker lid; lock the lid, ensuring steam-release valve and quick-release button are up. Select **PRESSURE COOK** low heat and set time for 4 minutes. Taking care, quick-release the pressure. Allow to stand for 10 minutes before removing the lid; this will result in perfectly cooked rice.
4 Serve ratatouille rice topped with goat cheese and extra basil leaves.

MEXICAN RICE WITH CHORIZO, POTATO & JALAPEÑO

Prep 10 mins   **Sauté** 5 mins   **Pressure Cook** 15 mins   **Serves** 4   Gluten-free

3 fresh jalapeño chiles
1 bunch cilantro
3 garlic cloves, crushed
3 tsp ground cumin
2 tbsp extra virgin olive oil
½lb (250g) chorizo sausages,
   casings removed, cut into ½in
   (1cm) pieces (see tip)
1 medium red onion, about 6oz
   (170g), finely chopped
¾lb (400g) red potatoes, cut into
   ½in (1cm) cubes
2 corn cobs (800g), kernels removed
2 cups (400g) long-grain rice, rinsed
1⅔cups (400ml) gluten-free
   chicken stock
3½oz (100g) feta cheese, crumbled
to serve: hot sauce and lime wedges

1 Remove seeds from jalapeño chiles and finely chop. Chop three-quarters of the cilantro, including the stems. Place jalapeño, chopped cilantro, garlic, cumin, 1 tablespoon cold water, and 1 tablespoon of the oil in a medium bowl. Using a hand-held blender, blend to a smooth paste; season with salt.

2 Select **SAUTÉ** high heat and preheat for 5 minutes. When the inner pot is hot, add remaining oil, the chorizo, and onion; **SAUTÉ**, stirring, for 4 minutes. Add potato and corn kernels; **SAUTÉ**, stirring, for a further 1 minute. Add rice and jalapeño paste; stir to coat grains. Turn off **SAUTÉ**. Add stock to the inner pot. Cover with the pressure-cooker lid; lock the lid, ensuring steam-release valve and quick-release button are up. Select **PRESSURE COOK** low heat and set time for 15 minutes.

3 Meanwhile, chop remaining cilantro.

4 Taking care, quick-release the pressure. Serve rice topped with chopped cilantro, feta, and hot sauce, with lime wedges on the side for squeezing over.

TIP To ensure this recipe is gluten-free, check the ingredients list for the chorizo before purchasing and buy gluten-free chicken stock.

SQUASH, SAGE & GOAT CHEESE RISOTTO

Prep 20 mins   **Sauté** 21 mins   **Pressure Cook** 7 mins   **Serves** 4
Gluten-free   Good to freeze   Vegetarian

2¼lb (1kg) Kabocha squash
4 tbsp (60g) butter
2 tbsp extra virgin olive oil
1 large onion, about 7oz (200g),
    finely chopped
4 garlic cloves, crushed
1 tbsp finely chopped sage
2 cups (400g) arborio rice
½ cup (125ml) dry white wine
6 cups (1.5lt) gluten-free
    vegetable stock
½ cup (40g) grated Parmesan-style
    vegetarian cheese
¼ cup (60ml) whipping cream
¼ cup (60ml) lemon juice
½ cup (60g) fresh goat cheese,
    crumbled
to serve: extra finely grated
    Parmesan-style vegetarian
    cheese and extra sage
    leaves, fried

1 Cut four ½in (1.5cm)-thick wedges from the squash with the skin on; remove and discard seeds. Peel, seed, and cut remaining squash into 1in (2.5cm) pieces.

2 Select **SAUTÉ** high heat and preheat for 5 minutes. When the inner pot is hot, add butter. Once butter is melted, add the squash wedges and **SAUTÉ** for 3 minutes on each side or until browned. Transfer wedges to a plate. Add squash pieces to the inner pot and **SAUTÉ** for 8 minutes, turning occasionally, or until golden. Using a slotted spoon, transfer squash pieces to plate.

3 Add oil to the inner pot, then add onion and garlic; **SAUTÉ**, stirring, for 4 minutes until softened. Add sage and rice; **SAUTÉ**, stirring, for a further 2 minutes or until rice is translucent. Add wine and **SAUTÉ** for 1 minute.

4 Return squash pieces to the inner pot. Stir in stock and place squash wedges on top. Cover with the pressure-cooker lid; lock the lid, ensuring steam-release valve and quick-release button are up. Select **PRESSURE COOK** low heat and set time for 7 minutes.

5 Taking care, quick-release the pressure. Carefully transfer squash wedges to a plate. Stir Parmesan cheese, cream, lemon juice, and half of the goat cheese into the risotto; season with salt and pepper to taste.

6 Serve risotto topped with remaining goat cheese, squash wedges, extra grated Parmesan cheese, and fried sage leaves.

33

SHRIMP BIBIMBAP

Prep 10 mins   **Sauté** 8 mins   **Pressure Cook** 15 mins   **Serves** 4   Dairy-free   Pescatarian

---

¼ cup (65g) gochujang (Korean chili paste) (see tip on page 12)

2 eggs

2 garlic cloves, crushed

1lb (500g) large shrimp, peeled, deveined, butterflied

2 tbsp sesame oil

1 large carrot, about 10oz (300g), cut into julienne

2 medium zucchini, about 8½ oz (240g), cut into julienne

2 cups (400g) sushi rice, rinsed, drained

1 tbsp mirin

1 tbsp soy sauce

2 cups (160g) bean sprouts

to serve: sliced spring onion (scallion) and white sesame seeds

1 Select **SAUTÉ** high heat and preheat for 5 minutes. Whisk 2 teaspoons of the gochujang and the eggs in a bowl. Combine another 2 teaspoons of gochujang, half of the garlic, and the shrimp in another bowl.

2 When the inner pot is hot, add 2 teaspoons of the sesame oil. Pour in egg mixture; tilt pot to swirl over base to cover; **SAUTÉ** for 2 minutes. Using a spatula, carefully flip omelet and **SAUTÉ** for 30 seconds. Transfer to a plate.

3 Add 2 teaspoons sesame oil to the inner pot, then add shrimp; **SAUTÉ**, stirring, for 3 minutes until opaque. Transfer to a plate.

4 Add 2 teaspoons sesame oil to the inner pot, then add carrot; **SAUTÉ**, stirring, for 1 minute or until slightly softened. Season with salt. Transfer to a plate. Repeat cooking with zucchini.

5 Add rice and remaining garlic to the inner pot; stir until grains are coated. Turn off **SAUTÉ**. Pour in 1⅔ cups (400ml) water. Cover with the pressure-cooker lid; lock the lid, ensuring the steam-release valve and quick-release button are up. Select **PRESSURE COOK** low heat and set time for 15 minutes.

6 Meanwhile, roll up omelet; slice into thin strips. Combine remaining gochujang, the mirin, and soy sauce in a bowl.

7 Taking care, quick-release the pressure. Top rice with shrimp, omelet strips, carrot, and zucchini. Cover again with the pressure-cooker lid. Allow to stand for 10 minutes to warm through.

8 Serve shrimp bibimbap topped with bean sprouts, spring onion, and sesame seeds; drizzle with the gochujang sauce mixture.

TIP Don't depressurize naturally or the rice will be overcooked.

JOLLOF RICE WITH CHICKEN

Prep 10 mins   **Sauté** 15 mins   **Pressure Cook** 13 mins   **Serves** 4–6
Gluten-free   Dairy-free   Good to freeze

2½lb (1.2kg) chicken drumsticks
2 tbsp extra virgin olive oil
1 medium red onion, about 6oz
   (170g), thinly sliced
2 garlic cloves, crushed
1 habanero chile, seeded,
   finely chopped
1 tbsp tomato purée
2 tsp curry powder
1 tbsp thyme leaves
1 cinnamon stick
2 bay leaves
14.5 oz (411g) can diced tomatoes
2 cups (500ml) gluten-free
   chicken stock
2 cups (360g) basmati rice,
   rinsed thoroughly
¾ lb (300g) green beans, cut into
   1in (2.5cm) lengths
to serve: lime cheeks

1 Select **SAUTÉ** high heat and preheat for 5 minutes. Season chicken with salt and pepper.
2 When the inner pot is hot, add half of the oil, then add half of the chicken; **SAUTÉ**, turning occasionally, for 5 minutes or until browned. Transfer to a plate. Repeat with remaining oil and chicken; transfer to plate.
3 Add onion to the inner pot and **SAUTÉ**, stirring occasionally, for 3 minutes or until softened. Add garlic, chile, tomato purée, curry powder, thyme, cinnamon, and bay leaves; **SAUTÉ**, stirring, for a further 2 minutes or until fragrant. Add tomatoes and stock, then return chicken and any resting juices to the inner pot; season with salt and pepper to taste. Turn off **SAUTÉ**.

4 Cover with the pressure-cooker lid; lock the lid, ensuring steam-release valve and quick-release button are up. Select **PRESSURE COOK** high heat and set time for 10 minutes. Taking care, quick-release the pressure. Transfer chicken to a plate and cover to keep warm. Reserve cooking liquid.
5 Place rice, green beans, and 2½ cups (625ml) of cooking liquid in the inner pot. Cover with the pressure-cooker lid. Select **PRESSURE COOK** high heat and set time for 3 minutes. Naturally release for 10 minutes, then, taking care, quick-release the pressure. Fluff up the rice and season to taste.
6 Serve rice mixture with chicken, remaining cooking liquid, and lime cheeks.

37

CLAYPOT CHICKEN

Prep 20 mins   **Pressure Cook** 4 mins   **Serves** 4   Dairy-free   Good to freeze

2 tsp sesame oil

2 tbsp oyster sauce

2 tbsp soy sauce

1 tbsp Shaohsing rice wine

1 tbsp light soft brown sugar

2 tbsp finely grated fresh ginger

2½ lb (1.2kg) boneless, skinless
   chicken thighs, trimmed

¼ cup (25g) dried shiitake
   mushrooms

1 cup (250ml) boiling water

1 chicken bouillon cube, crumbled

⅓ cup finely chopped cilantro stems
   and roots, leaves reserved for
   serving

6 spring onions (scallions),
   thinly sliced

4 star anise

2 cups (500ml) chicken stock

2 cups (400g) medium-grain rice

¾ lb (400g) gai lan or broccolini, cut
   into 2 in (5cm) lengths

1 Combine sesame oil, oyster sauce, soy sauce, rice wine, sugar, and ginger in a bowl; add chicken and allow to marinate for 10 minutes.

2 Meanwhile, place mushrooms in a small bowl; pour over the 1 cup (250ml) boiling water and allow to stand for 10 minutes or until mushrooms are softened. Remove mushrooms and finely slice; reserve soaking liquid.

3 Line bottom and side of the inner pot with parchment paper; this will prevent food from catching on the bottom and the appliance turning off. Put chicken and its marinade, sliced mushrooms, mushroom soaking liquid, bouillon cube, cilantro stems and roots, spring onion, star anise, stock, rice, and gai lan or broccolini in the inner pot. Cover with the pressure-cooker lid; lock the lid, ensuring steam-release valve and quick-release button are up. Select **PRESSURE COOK** low heat and set time for 4 minutes. Taking care, quick-release the pressure.

4 Serve chicken and rice mixture topped with reserved cilantro leaves.

SLOW COOK

Set-and-forget cooking has never been simpler. Transform tougher cuts of meat and seafood into hearty casseroles, stews, and curries, or indulge your sweet tooth with delectable desserts.

SPANISH-STYLE BRAISED CHICKEN & BROAD BEANS

Prep 10 mins **Sauté** 30 mins **Slow Cook** 4 hrs **Serves** 4 Dairy-free Good to freeze

3½ lb (1.4kg) Maryland-cut chicken
 (including drumstick and thigh)
1 tbsp sweet paprika
¼ cup (60ml) extra virgin olive oil
½ lb (200g) pancetta, finely chopped
6 shallots, about 5½oz (150g) in
 total, thinly sliced
3 garlic cloves, thinly sliced
1 bay leaf
1 lb (500g) frozen fava beans, thawed
1 cup (250ml) dry white wine
1 cup (250ml) chicken stock
to serve: flat-leaf parsley leaves and
 toasted crusty bread

1 Select **SAUTÉ** high heat and preheat for 5 minutes. Place chicken and paprika in a large bowl; toss to coat. Season with salt and pepper.
2 When the inner pot is hot, add 1 tablespoon of the oil and half of the chicken; **SAUTÉ**, turning occasionally, for 6 minutes or until golden brown. Transfer to a plate. Repeat with another 1 tablespoon of the oil and remaining chicken; transfer to plate.
3 Add pancetta, shallots, garlic, bay leaf, and remaining oil to the inner pot; **SAUTÉ**, stirring occasionally, for 5 minutes or until shallots are softened. Add fava beans, white wine, and stock;
bring to a simmer, stirring with a wooden spoon to release flavors from the bottom of the pot. Return chicken to the inner pot.
4 Cover with pressure-cooker lid. Select **SLOW COOK** low heat and set time for 4 hours; **SLOW COOK** until chicken is tender.
5 Using a slotted spoon, transfer chicken and bean mixture to a serving dish; cover to keep warm. Select **SAUTÉ** high heat. Simmer cooking liquid for 10 minutes or until reduced.
6 Pour reduced sauce over chicken and scatter with parsley leaves. Serve with crusty bread.

TIP Chicken can also be slow-cooked on high for 2 hours.

CHOCOLATE HAZELNUT CHEESECAKE

Prep 30 mins (+ standing & refrigeration)   **Slow Cook** 2 hrs   **Serves** 10   Good to freeze

½ lb (250g) chocolate
  sandwich cookies
6 tbsp (80g) butter, melted
2 x 8oz (225g) packages cream
  cheese, softened
½ cup (110g) sugar
26.5oz (750g) jar chocolate
  hazelnut spread
3 eggs
2 tbsp skinless roasted hazelnuts,
  coarsely chopped

1 Grease an 8in (20cm) round springform pan; line with parchment paper. Make sure the pan fits in the inner pot without touching the sides; remove pan. Place the wire rack in the inner pot. Cover with the pressure-cooker lid. Select **SLOW COOK** high heat and set time for 20 minutes to preheat.

2 Process sandwich cookies to fine crumbs; add butter and process until combined. Press mixture into the bottom of the lined pan and smooth the surface with a spoon. Place in the freezer for 5 minutes.

3 Process cream cheese and sugar in a clean food processor until smooth and combined. Add 1½ cups (500g) of the chocolate hazelnut spread and process until combined. With motor operating, add 1 egg at a time, processing until combined.

4 Add 1 cup (250ml) water to the inner pot. Pour filling mixture over biscuit base in the pan. Taking care, place pan on the rack in the inner pot.

5 Cover the inner pot with a clean kitchen towel, then cover with the pressure-cooker lid, wrapping the kitchen towel over the lid. Select **SLOW COOK** high heat and set time for 2 hours.

6 Turn off the appliance. Allow cheesecake to stand inside covered appliance for 1 hour. Remove the pan from the inner pot; allow to stand for 30 minutes. Cover and refrigerate for 4 hours or until cold.

7 Before serving, combine remaining chocolate hazelnut spread with water in a heatproof bowl; whisk until smooth. Serve cheesecake topped with the sauce and hazelnuts.

45

SLOW-COOKED GINGER PORK BELLY & CABBAGE

Prep 10 mins   **Sauté** 9 mins   **Slow Cook** 2 hrs   **Serves** 4   Dairy-free   Good to freeze

1 tbsp sesame oil

2¼ lb (1kg) pork belly, cut into ½in (1cm)-thick pieces lengthwise

6 spring onions (scallions), cut into 2-in (4cm) lengths

4 garlic cloves, crushed

1 tbsp finely grated fresh ginger

2 tbsp gochujang (Korean chili paste) (see tips)

2 cups (500ml) chicken stock

1 tbsp rice wine vinegar

2 tbsp soy sauce

1 tbsp sugar

½ small Napa or Savoy cabbage (400g), cut into 1-in (2.5cm)-thick slices

to serve: toasted sesame seeds, extra sliced spring onion (scallion), and steamed rice (optional)

1 Select **SAUTÉ** high heat and preheat for 5 minutes. When the inner pot is hot, add sesame oil, then add pork; **SAUTÉ** for 2 minutes on each side or until browned. Transfer pork to a plate.

2 Add spring onions, garlic, ginger, and gochujang to the inner pot; **SAUTÉ**, stirring, for 1 minute. Add stock, vinegar, soy sauce, and sugar; stir to combine. Return pork to the inner pot and turn to coat in the mixture. Place cabbage on top of pork. Turn off **SAUTÉ**.

3 Cover with the pressure-cooker lid. Select **SLOW COOK** high heat and set time for 2 hours; **SLOW COOK** until pork is tender and falling apart.

4 Scatter pork with sesame seeds and extra spring onion. Serve with rice, if you like.

TIP Gochujang is a spicy Korean red chili paste available from larger supermarkets and Asian grocers.

LAMB KLEFTIKO WITH POTATOES

Prep 10 mins   **Sauté** 30 mins   **Slow Cook** 8 hrs   **Serves** 6
Dairy-free   Gluten-free   Good to freeze

2 tbsp extra virgin olive oil
3lb (1.4kg) bone-in lamb shoulder
   (see tips)
2¼lb (1kg) red and white baby
   potatoes, unpeeled, halved
1 large onion, about 7oz (200g),
   thinly sliced
2 dried bay leaves
1 cinnamon stick
⅓ cup (80ml) dry white wine
⅓ cup (80ml) gluten-free
   chicken stock
1 tbsp finely grated lemon zest
2 tbsp lemon juice
3 garlic cloves, crushed
1 tbsp dried oregano
⅓ cup (10g) fresh oregano leaves

1 Select **SAUTÉ** high heat and preheat for 5 minutes. When the inner pot is hot, add half of the oil, then add lamb; **SAUTÉ** for 20 minutes, turning every 5 minutes, until each side is well browned. Transfer lamb to a plate.

2 Add remaining oil to the inner pot, then add potatoes, onion, bay leaves, and cinnamon; **SAUTÉ**, stirring frequently, for 10 minutes or until potatoes are browned.

3 Place lamb on top of potatoes in the inner pot. Combine wine, stock, lemon zest and juice, garlic, and dried oregano in a medium bowl; pour over the lamb. Cover with the pressure-cooker lid. Select **SLOW COOK** low heat and set time for 8 hours; **SLOW COOK** until meat is falling off the bone.

4 Serve lamb and potatoes with the cooking liquid, scattered with fresh oregano leaves.

TIP Ensure the lamb shoulder will fit in the inner pot. If it doesn't fit, cut into large pieces.

OCTOPUS, FENNEL & SAFFRON STEW

Prep 15 mins **Sauté** 14 mins **Slow Cook** 4 hrs **Serves** 4
Dairy-free Gluten-free Pescatarian

2 tbsp extra virgin olive oil
2½ lb (1.2kg) octopus (or calamari)
   pieces, cleaned
2¼ lb (1kg) fennel bulbs, trimmed,
   cut into 1-in (2.5cm)-thick slices,
   fronds reserved
1 medium leek, about 12oz (350g),
   thinly sliced
4 garlic cloves, crushed
¾ cup (180ml) dry white wine
6 cups (1.5lt) gluten-free
   fish stock
3 bay leaves
½ tsp loosely packed saffron threads
to serve: crusty gluten-free bread

1 Select **SAUTÉ** high heat and preheat for 5 minutes. When the inner pot is hot, add 1 tablespoon of the oil, then add octopus; **SAUTÉ** for 2 minutes on each side or until browned. Transfer octopus to a plate.
2 Add remaining oil to the inner pot, then add fennel; **SAUTÉ** for 4 minutes, turning, until browned. Transfer fennel to a plate. Add leek and garlic to the inner pot; **SAUTÉ** for 1 minute. Add wine and **SAUTÉ** for a further 5 minutes or until reduced. Add stock, bay leaves, and saffron, then return octopus and fennel to the inner pot. Turn off **SAUTÉ**.
3 Cover with the pressure-cooker lid. Select **SLOW COOK** low heat and set time for 4 hours; **SLOW COOK** until octopus is very tender.
4 Serve with the cooking liquid and crusty bread, scattered with reserved fennel fronds.

RASPBERRY & WHITE CHOCOLATE WAFFLE DESSERT

Prep 10 mins   **Slow Cook** 4 hours   **Serves** 4–6

2 tbsp (30g) butter, melted
3 eggs
2 egg yolks
1 cup (250ml) milk
1 cup (225ml) heavy cream
1½ tbsp sugar
3 tsp finely grated lemon zest
1½ tsp vanilla extract
12oz (400g) round mini-waffles
2 cups (300g) frozen raspberries
3.5oz (100g) white chocolate,
  broken into chunks
to serve: vanilla ice cream

1 Grease a 7½in (19cm) round baking dish with melted butter. Add 1½ cups (375ml) water to the inner pot. Fold two lengths of aluminum foil into long strips and cross under the base of the dish to act as a sling. Using the sling, lower the dish into the inner pot.

2 To make the custard mixture, whisk together eggs, egg yolks, milk, cream, sugar, lemon zest, and vanilla extract in a large bowl until combined.

3 Layer a third of the waffles, raspberries, and chocolate in the dish. Repeat layering twice more. Pour over custard mixture, then gently press waffles into the mixture.

4 Cover with the pressure-cooker lid. Select **SLOW COOK** low heat and set time for 4 hours; **SLOW COOK** until custard is just set.

5 Using the sling, remove the dish from the inner pot. Serve with scoops of ice cream.

53

MEDITERRANEAN VEGGIES BRAISED IN OLIVE OIL

Prep 10 mins   **Sauté** 13 mins   **Slow Cook** 4 hrs   **Serves** 4   Pescatarian

2oz (55g) can anchovies in olive oil
½ cup (125ml) extra virgin olive oil
1 large onion, about 7oz (200g),
   thinly sliced
6 garlic cloves, bruised, peeled
1 lb (400g) green beans, trimmed
1 lb (400g) red bell peppers,
   deseeded, coarsely chopped
⅓ cup (12g) firmly packed
   oregano leaves
½ cup (12g) firmly packed flat-leaf
   parsley, coarsely chopped
1¼ lb (600g) fingerling potatoes,
   peeled, halved
28oz (793g) can crushed tomatoes
1 tsp sugar
1½ cups (180g) feta, crumbled
to serve: extra flat-leaf parsley
   leaves, extra virgin olive oil, and
   sourdough bread

1 Select **SAUTÉ** high heat and preheat for 5 minutes. Drain anchovies, reserving the oil; coarsely chop.
2 When the inner pot is hot, add reserved anchovy oil, the olive oil, and onion; **SAUTÉ**, stirring occasionally, for 5 minutes or until onion is slightly softened.
3 Add garlic, green beans, and red bell peppers to the inner pot; **SAUTÉ**, stirring occasionally, for 5 minutes or until softened. Add anchovies, oregano, and parsley; **SAUTÉ**, stirring, for a further 1 minute or until fragrant. Add potatoes, tomatoes, and sugar, then season with salt and pepper to taste; bring to a simmer.

Turn off **SAUTÉ**.
4 Cover with the pressure-cooker lid. Select **SLOW COOK** low heat and set time for 4 hours; **SLOW COOK** until vegetables are tender.
5 Top braised vegetables with feta and extra parsley leaves; drizzle with extra olive oil. Serve with sourdough bread for mopping up juices.

TIPS Omit the anchovies to make this dish vegetarian, and replace the feta with feta-style dairy-free cheese, too, for a vegan version.

Braised vegetables can also be cooked on high for 2 hours.

MASSAMAN BEEF CURRY

Prep 10 mins   **Sauté** 16 mins   **Slow Cook** 8 hours   **Serves** 6
Dairy-free   Gluten-free   Good to freeze

2 tbsp peanut oil
2 large onions, about 14oz (400g),
   cut into thin wedges
2¼ lb (1kg) beef stew meat cut into
   large pieces (see tip)
⅔ cup (200g) gluten-free
   massaman curry paste
2 x 13.5oz (400ml) cans
   coconut cream
6 cardamom pods, bruised
2 cinnamon sticks
4 star anise
2 bay leaves
2lb (900g) potatoes, peeled,
   cut into 2in (5cm) pieces
½ cup (70g) unsalted
   roasted peanuts
2 tbsp light soft brown sugar
2 tbsp gluten-free fish sauce
2 tbsp tamarind paste
⅓ cup (10g) cilantro leaves
to serve: steamed rice

1 Select **SAUTÉ** medium and preheat for 5 minutes. When the inner pot is hot, add half of the oil, then add onion; **SAUTÉ**, stirring, for 10 minutes or until lightly browned. Transfer onion to a plate.

2 Select **SAUTÉ** high heat. Add remaining oil to the inner pot, then add beef; **SAUTÉ** in batches, turning, for 5 minutes or until evenly browned. Add curry paste and **SAUTÉ**, stirring, for a further 1 minute or until fragrant.

3 Return onion to the inner pot with coconut milk, cardamom, cinnamon, star anise, bay leaves, potatoes, and peanuts. Cover with the pressure-cooker lid. Select **SLOW COOK** low heat and set time for 8 hours.

4 Stir brown sugar, fish sauce, and tamarind paste into curry at the end of the cooking time.

5 Top curry with cilantro leaves and serve with steamed rice.

TIP Other flavorful cuts of beef such as chuck or top blade are ideal for this recipe because of the long, slow cooking.

STEAM

Lock in moisture and steam chicken, fish, veggies, and puddings to perfection. Awaken your taste buds and try dumplings, broths, bread, and more—with wonderfully flavorful results.

STICKY TOFFEE PUDDINGS

Prep 10 mins (+ soaking)   **Steam** 25 mins   **Makes** 4   Good to freeze

8oz (225g) fresh medjool dates, pitted, chopped

1 tsp baking soda

1 tsp ground cinnamon

⅔ cup (150ml) boiling water

½ cup (125g) salted butter, melted, plus extra, to grease

1 tsp vanilla extract

2 eggs

1¼ cups (275g) firmly packed light soft brown sugar

1¼ cups (300ml) whipping cream

½ cup (50g) hazelnut meal

pinch of salt

1¼ cups (150g) flour

1¼ tsp baking powder

1 tsp salt

to serve: whipped cream (optional)

1 Put dates, baking soda, and ½ teaspoon of the cinnamon in a medium heatproof bowl; pour over ⅔ cup (150ml) boiling water. Cover and allow to stand for 30 minutes.

2 Meanwhile, grease four 1-cup (250ml) pudding molds or ramekins.

3 Break up dates with a fork, then stir in half the melted butter and the vanilla. Whisk in eggs, ½ cup (110g) of the sugar, and 2 tablespoons of the cream until well combined. Season with the pinch of salt. Fold in the hazelnut meal and flour until just combined. Divide mixture among dishes. Cover each with a disc of parchment paper then aluminum foil, pressing firmly into the side of each dish. Add 2 cups (500ml) water to the inner pot. Lower dishes into the pot.

4 Cover with the pressure-cooker lid; lock the lid, ensuring steam-release valve and quick-release button are up. Select **STEAM** high heat and set time for 25 minutes.

5 Meanwhile, to make the caramel sauce, combine the remaining melted butter and sugar over a low heat in a heavy-based saucepan. Stir occasionally for 5 minutes until sugar is dissolved and mixture is bubbly. Stir in remaining cinnamon and cream. Increase heat to medium and simmer for 5 minutes or until slightly thickened.

6 Taking care, quick-release the pressure. Remove puddings from the inner pot and invert into bowls. Serve warm with caramel sauce and whipped cream, if you like.

TIP Make one large pudding using a 6-cup (1.5-liter) pudding bowl, and steaming for 32 minutes.

STEAMED SALMON & CABBAGE WITH ASIAN BROTH

Prep 10 mins   **Steam** 2 mins   **Serves** 4   Dairy-free   Pescatarian

2 cups (500ml) fish stock

3-in (7cm) piece of fresh ginger, peeled, thinly sliced

1 cinnamon stick

2 tbsp yakitori sauce

2 tbsp Shaohsing rice wine

3½ oz (100g) fresh shiitake mushrooms, halved if large

6 spring onions (scallions), cut into 1½ in (4cm) lengths

½ small Napa or Savoy cabbage, about 14oz (400g), cut into 1¼ in (3cm)-thick slices

4 x 8oz (225g) salmon fillets, skinned

8oz (200g) package shelled baby edamame

1 tbsp sesame seeds

1 tsp sesame oil

3 red radishes, cut into matchsticks

2 tbsp pickled ginger

1 Place stock, ginger, cinnamon, yakitori sauce, rice wine, mushrooms, and spring onions in the inner pot. Arrange cabbage in a single layer in the pot. Place the wire rack on top of the cabbage, then place salmon in a single layer on top of that. Cover with the pressure-cooker lid; lock the lid, ensuring steam-release valve and quick-release button are up. Select **STEAM** high heat and set time for 2 minutes.

2 Taking care, quick-release the pressure. Gently remove salmon and cabbage from the inner pot. Strain cooking liquid into a jug, then pour ½ cup (125ml) into each of 4 serving bowls. Divide cabbage, salmon, and edamame evenly among bowls. Combine sesame seeds, sesame oil, radishes, and pickled ginger in a small bowl. Serve broth topped with sesame-radish mixture.

BANG BANG CHICKEN SALAD

Prep 20 mins　**Steam** 4 mins　**Serves** 4　Dairy-free

4 spring onions (scallions)
½ cup (125ml) chicken stock
4 star anise
2 tsp Sichuan peppercorns
½ cup (20g) dried shiitake
　mushrooms
1 lb (450g) boneless, skinless
　chicken breasts
2 tsp sesame oil
1 tbsp Chinkiang vinegar (see tip)
1 tbsp soy sauce
1 tsp sugar
1 tbsp peanut oil
1 cup (50g) snow pea tendrils or
　other pea shoots
3½ oz (100g) snow peas, blanched,
　shredded
4 baby cucumbers, seeds removed,
　coarsely chopped
¼ cup (35g) unsalted roasted
　peanuts, coarsely chopped
to serve: chili oil

1 Coarsely chop 3 of the spring onions and place in the inner pot with chicken stock, star anise, Sichuan peppercorns, and mushrooms. Place the wire rack in the inner pot, then place chicken in a single layer on top. Cover with the pressure-cooker lid; lock the lid, ensuring steam-release valve and quick-release button are up. Select **STEAM** high heat and set time for 4 minutes.
2 Taking care, quick-release the pressure. Transfer chicken to a plate to cool. Strain cooking liquid into a small bowl; remove the mushrooms and allow to cool slightly. Add sesame oil, vinegar, soy sauce, sugar, and oil to the bowl; whisk until evenly combined.
3 Shred chicken and place in a large bowl. Thinly slice the mushrooms and remaining spring onion; add to the chicken with pea tendrils, shredded snow peas, and cucumber. Pour over dressing and toss to combine. Serve chicken salad scattered with peanuts and drizzled with chili oil.

TIP Chinese Chinkiang or black rice vinegar is made from glutinous rice and has a malty, sweet flavor. It is available from Asian grocers.

STEAMED EGGPLANT WITH BLACK VINEGAR DRESSING

Prep 10 mins **Sauté** 3 mins **Steam** 6 mins **Serves** 4 Dairy-free Vegetarian

3 tsp sesame oil
2 garlic cloves, crushed
2in (5cm) piece of fresh ginger, cut
   into julienne
1 tsp freshly ground pepper
¼ cup (60ml) Chinkiang vinegar
1½ tbsp sugar
1½ tbsp soy sauce
1¼ lb (600g) Japanese eggplants,
   halved lengthwise
1 long red chile, cut into matchsticks
1½ tbsp white sesame seeds,
   toasted
to serve: cilantro leaves

1 To make the dressing, select **SAUTÉ** high heat and preheat for 5 minutes. When the inner pot is hot, add sesame oil, garlic, ginger, and pepper; **SAUTÉ**, stirring, for 2 minutes or until fragrant. Add vinegar, sugar, soy sauce, and ¼ cup (60ml) water; **SAUTÉ**, stirring, for a further 1 minute or until sugar dissolves. Transfer dressing to a small bowl.
2 Add 1 cup (250ml) water to the inner pot. Place the wire rack in the pot, then place eggplant in a single layer on top. Cover with the pressure-cooker lid; lock the lid, ensuring steam-release valve and quick-release button are up.

Select **STEAM** high heat and set time for 6 minutes.
3 Taking care, quick-release the pressure. Transfer eggplant to a platter; drizzle with the black vinegar dressing and scatter with chile, sesame seeds, and cilantro leaves. Serve hot or at room temperature.

TIP Do not depressurize naturally or leave the eggplant sitting in the appliance, as this will cause the eggplant to be overcooked.

STEAMED VEGGIE DUMPLINGS

Prep 15 mins   **Sauté** 5 mins   **Steam** 3 mins   **Makes** 24
Dairy-free   Good to freeze   Vegetarian

8oz (225g) baby spinach leaves
1 tbsp vegetable oil
8oz (225g) oyster mushrooms
   (or shiitake or a mixture; discard
   shiitake stems), chopped
1½ tsp finely grated fresh
   ginger
1 bunch chives, about 1½oz (15g),
   cut into 1in (2.5cm) pieces
2 spring onions (scallions),
   finely chopped
2 tbsp vegetarian oyster sauce
   or stir-fry sauce
24 round dumpling (pot-sticker)
   or gyoza wrappers
to serve: chili crisp

1 Put spinach in a heatproof bowl and pour over enough boiling water to cover. Allow to stand for 30 seconds or until spinach wilts. Drain, then squeeze out excess liquid.

2 Select **SAUTÉ** high heat and preheat for 5 minutes. When the inner pot is hot, add oil, then mushrooms; **SAUTÉ**, stirring, for 4 minutes. Add ginger, chives, and spring onions; **SAUTÉ** for a further 1 minute. Stir in sauce and spinach. Turn off the appliance. Transfer spinach mixture to a bowl and set aside to cool. Wash the inner pot and return to the appliance.

3 Working in batches, place 3 teaspoons filling in the center of each wrapper. Using your fingertips, moisten the edge of each wrapper with a little water. Fold in half, then pinch the middle and make four pleats on each side. Repeat with remaining wrappers

and filling to make 24 dumplings in total.

4 Fill the inner pot with ¾ cup (180ml) water and insert the air-fryer basket. Layer half of the dumplings over the bottom of the basket, then place perforated tray on top. Place remaining dumplings in a single layer on the tray. Cover with the pressure-cooker lid; lock the lid, ensuring the steam-release valve and quick-release button are up. Select **STEAM** high heat and set time for 3 minutes.

5 Taking care, quick-release the pressure. Arrange dumplings on a platter and serve with chili crisp.

TIPS Chili crisp is a chili oil with crispy Asian shallots.

Do not depressurize naturally or leave the dumplings sitting in the appliance, or they will overcook.

SMOKED CHEDDAR SODA BREAD

Prep 15 mins **Steam** 50 mins **Roast** 10 mins **Serves** 8

1¾ cups (240g) whole wheat flour
2 cups (300g) white spelt flour
1½ tsp baking powder
1½ tsp baking soda
1 tsp sea salt flakes
6 tbsp (80g) butter, finely chopped
2 cups (240g) coarsely grated
    smoked Cheddar
about 1½ cups (375ml) buttermilk,
    plus extra for brushing
½ cup (75g) mixed seeds (see tips)
olive oil cooking oil spray

CHILI BUTTER
½ cup (125g) butter, softened
½ cup (125g) Sriracha mayonnaise

1 Grease a deep 8in (20cm) round cake tin; line with parchment paper.
2 Sift flours, baking powder, baking soda, and salt into a large bowl. Using your fingertips, rub in butter, then stir in Cheddar. Add enough of the buttermilk to mix to a dough. Gently knead on a floured work surface until just smooth. Shape into a 6½in (17cm) round and flatten the top. Sprinkle a third of the seeds over the bottom of the pan, then place dough round in pan. Brush top with extra buttermilk; sprinkle with remaining seeds. Make a shallow crisscross cut on top of the dough. Cover pan with aluminum foil, securing with string. Use extra string to make a handle.
3 Add 2 cups (500ml) water to the inner pot, then place the wire rack in the pot. Place pan on top of the rack. Cover with the pressure-cooker lid; lock the lid, ensuring steam-release valve and quick-release button are up. Select **STEAM** high heat and set time for 50 minutes.
4 Taking care, quick-release the pressure. Remove pan and rack from the inner pot. Transfer bread, top-side up, to rack and spray all over with oil. Place the bread on rack back in inner pot. Cover with the air-fryer lid. Select **ROAST** and set temperature to 350°F/180°C and time for 10 minutes; **ROAST** until bread is golden.
5 To make the chili butter, beat butter and mayonnaise with an electric mixer until light and fluffy. Serve with warm slices of the bread.

TIPS We used ⅓ cup (75g) toasted sesame seeds and 1 tablespoon each of poppy, fennel, and cumin seeds and sea salt flakes. Bread will keep for 3 days or for up to 1 month if frozen.

PRESSURE COOK

Use this function to speed-cook your way to fabulous flavors. Try traditionally slow-cooked cuts of meat and ragù for meltingly tender results, as well as soups and creamy custard that melts in the mouth.

SAUSAGE & BEEF RAGÙ

Prep 10 mins   **Sauté** 20 mins   **Pressure Cook** 20 mins   **Serves** 6   Good to freeze

1lb (450g) Italian-style fresh
   pork sausages
2 tbsp extra virgin olive oil
1lb (450g) lean ground beef
3 garlic cloves, crushed
1 medium onion, about (5½oz) 150g,
   finely chopped
1 medium carrot, about (4oz) 120g,
   finely chopped
1 celery stalk, about (5½oz) 150g,
   finely chopped
⅓ cup (95g) tomato purée
2 tsp Italian-style dried herbs
⅓ cup (80ml) red wine (optional)
⅔ cup (160ml) beef stock
2 x 14.5oz (411g) cans
   diced tomatoes
2 bay leaves
¼ cup (7g) finely chopped
   flat-leaf parsley
to serve: pasta of choice and finely
   grated Parmesan cheese

1 Squeeze the sausage meat from the casings and roll into walnut-sized meatballs; discard casings.
2 Select **SAUTÉ** high heat and preheat for 5 minutes. When the inner pot is hot, add 1 tablespoon of the oil, then add the ground beef; **SAUTÉ** for 8 minutes, breaking up with a wooden spoon, until browned. Using a slotted spoon, transfer ground beef to a plate. Add remaining oil to the inner pot, then add the meatballs; **SAUTÉ** for 2 minutes, stirring, until browned. Using a slotted spoon, transfer meatballs to plate.
3 Add garlic, onion, carrot, and celery to the inner pot; **SAUTÉ**, stirring, for 8 minutes. Add tomato purée; **SAUTÉ** for a further 2 minutes. Return beef and meatballs to the inner pot. Stir in dried herbs and wine, if you like, or ⅓ cup of water; bring to a boil.
4 Add stock, tomatoes, and bay leaves to the inner pot; stir well. Cover with the pressure-cooker lid; lock the lid, ensuring steam-release valve and quick-release button are up. Select **PRESSURE COOK** low heat and set time for 20 minutes.
5 Taking care, quick-release the pressure. Stir parsley into ragù. Serve ragù with your favorite pasta, sprinkled with grated Parmesan cheese.

MEXICAN SLOW-COOKED PULLED PORK (CARNITAS)

Prep 15 mins   **Sauté** 40 mins   **Pressure Cook** 1 hr   **Makes** 8   Good to freeze

---

5½lb (2.5kg) boneless pork shoulder, halved, skin removed
1 tbsp ground cumin
1 tbsp ground coriander
3 tsp fine sea salt
2 tsp dried oregano
1 cup (250ml) orange juice
1 cup (250ml) chicken stock
2 medium red onions, about 12oz (340g) in total, thinly sliced
1 jalapeño chile, finely chopped
½ cup (25g) finely chopped cilantro roots and stems
4 garlic cloves, crushed
1 cinnamon stick
2 tbsp extra virgin olive oil
8 x 8-inch soft flour tortillas, about 14oz (384g) in total
to serve: sour cream, sliced pickled jalapeños, hot sauce, chopped cilantro leaves, and lime wedges

1 Pat pork dry with kitchen paper. Rub the outside with combined cumin, coriander, sea salt, and oregano.

2 Put orange juice, stock, onion, chili, cilantro roots and stems, garlic, and cinnamon in the inner pot; place pork on top. Cover with the pressure-cooker lid; lock the lid, ensuring steam-release valve and quick-release button are up. Select **PRESSURE COOK** high heat and set time for 1 hour.

3 Naturally release the pressure; this will take about 5 minutes. Transfer pork to a bowl and cover to keep warm.

4 Select **SAUTÉ** high heat and set time for 30 minutes; **SAUTÉ**, stirring occasionally, until sauce is reduced and thickened. Transfer sauce to a bowl. Carefully wipe the inner pot clean.

5 Shred pork using two forks. Select **SAUTÉ** high heat. Add oil to the inner pot, then add shredded meat; **SAUTÉ** for 10 minutes, stirring frequently, until meat is crisped. Add 2 cups (500ml) reduced sauce to the inner pot and stir to coat the meat.

6 Warm tortillas in a frying pan or wrap in aluminum foil and warm in the oven. Spoon sour cream onto tortillas, then top with pulled pork, pickled jalapeños, hot sauce, and cilantro leaves. Serve with lime wedges for squeezing over.

JERK LAMB SHANKS

Prep 10 mins   **Sauté** 18 mins   **Pressure Cook** 40 mins   **Serves** 4   Dairy-free   Good to freeze

5lb (2.2kg) lamb shanks
2½ tbsp mild jerk paste
1 tbsp flour
2 tbsp extra virgin olive oil
1 medium red onion, about 6oz
   (170g), thinly sliced
3 garlic cloves, thinly sliced
2 bay leaves
½ cup (125ml) red wine
2 cups (500ml) beef stock
15oz (425g) can black beans,
   drained, rinsed
1lb (450g) cherry tomatoes
to serve: sliced cilantro leaves and
   coconut rice (see tip)

1 Select **SAUTÉ** high heat and preheat for 5 minutes. Put lamb in a large bowl and rub with jerk paste until well coated, then toss in flour. When the inner pot is hot, add oil, then add lamb; **SAUTÉ**, turning occasionally, for 10 minutes or until lamb is browned. Transfer lamb to a plate.
2 Add onion, garlic, and bay leaves to the inner pot; **SAUTÉ**, stirring, for 3 minutes or until slightly softened. Add red wine and stock. Using a wooden spoon, scrape up any bits from the bottom of the pot, then return lamb to the inner pot.
3 Cover with the pressure-cooker lid; lock the lid, ensuring steam-release valve and quick-release button are up. Select **PRESSURE COOK** high heat and set time for 40 minutes.
4 Taking care, quick-release the pressure. Transfer lamb to a plate and cover to keep warm.

Add beans and tomatoes to the inner pot. Select **SAUTÉ** high heat and set cook time for 20 minutes; **SAUTÉ**, stirring occasionally, until sauce is slightly thickened. Discard bay leaves and season to taste. Return lamb to the inner pot and stir to coat in bean mixture.
5 Top jerk lamb with cilantro and serve with coconut rice.

TIP To make coconut rice, put 1½ cups (300g) jasmine rice, 1 tablespoon dried unsweetened coconut, 1 teaspoon salt, and 1 cup (250ml) each of coconut milk and water in the inner pot. Cover with the pressure-cooker lid. Select **PRESSURE COOK** high heat and set time for 3 minutes. Naturally release the pressure for 10 minutes, then press down quick-release button until it clicks. Allow pot to depressurize, then remove lid.

CHICKEN PHO

Prep 10 mins   **Sauté** 10 mins   **Pressure Cook** 30 mins   **Serves** 4   Dairy-free

olive oil cooking spray
4 shallots, thinly sliced
1¼in (3cm) piece of fresh ginger,
   peeled, sliced
4 garlic cloves, bruised
2 cinnamon sticks
4 star anise
1 tsp fennel seeds
1 tbsp Chinese chicken bouillon
   powder (see tips)
4 cups (1 liter) hot water
3½lb (1.4kg) Maryland-cut chicken
   (including drumstick and thigh)
1 liter (4 cups) coconut water
¼ cup (60ml) fish sauce, or to taste
8oz (225g) pho dried rice noodles
   (see tips)
1 cup (80g) bean sprouts
2 spring onions (scallions),
   thinly sliced
2 cups (about 60g) mixed fresh
   herbs, such as cilantro, Thai basil,
   and Vietnamese mint, roughly torn
1 medium lemon, about 5oz (140g),
   cut into wedges
to serve: hoisin sauce, Sriracha, and
   sliced red chile

1 Select **SAUTÉ** high heat and preheat for 5 minutes. When the inner pot is hot, spray base with oil, then add shallots, ginger, garlic, cinnamon, star anise, and fennel seeds; **SAUTÉ**, stirring, for 10 minutes or until golden and well toasted.
2 Meanwhile, combine bouillon powder and the 4 cups (1 liter) hot water in a bowl.
3 Add chicken, chicken stock, and coconut water to the inner pot. Cover with the pressure-cooker lid; lock the lid, ensuring steam-release valve and quick-release button are up. Select **PRESSURE COOK** high heat and set time for 30 minutes.
4 Taking care, quick-release the pressure. Using a slotted spoon, transfer chicken to a bowl. Once cool enough to handle, remove skin and bones, then shred chicken into large pieces. Keep chicken warm until needed.
5 Drain soup into a large saucepan; discard solids. Stir in fish sauce and keep soup warm.
6 Cook noodles according to the package directions. Drain, then divide among 4 bowls; top with shredded chicken, bean sprouts, spring onions, and herbs. Pour or ladle over the soup. Serve pho with lemon wedges, hoisin sauce, Sriracha, and sliced chile.

TIPS Chinese chicken bouillon powder has a more concentrated flavor than ordinary stock cubes. You can find it at Asian grocers and supermarkets.

Pho noodles are flat, wide rice noodles.

Do not depressurize naturally or the chicken will be overcooked.

CREMA CATALANA WITH CHERRIES

Prep 10 mins (+ standing & refrigeration)   **Sauté** 2 mins   **Pressure Cook** 15 mins
Makes 4   Gluten-free

1½ cups (375ml) heavy cream
¾ cup (180ml) milk
4 strips of lemon rind
4 strips of orange rind
1 cinnamon stick
1 tsp vanilla extract
$1/8$ tsp saffron threads
6 egg yolks
¾ cup (165g) sugar, plus
    extra ⅓ cup (75g)
1 tbsp gluten-free cornstarch
1 cup (250ml) boiling water
4oz (125g) cherries
8oz (250g) raspberries

1 Put cream, milk, citrus rinds, cinnamon, vanilla, and saffron in the inner pot. Select **SAUTÉ** high heat and set time to 2 minutes. Turn off **SAUTÉ**. Allow the cream mixture to stand in the inner pot for 15 minutes to infuse.

2 Whisk egg yolks, the ¾ cup (165g) sugar, and the cornstarch in a medium bowl until pale and thickened. Strain cream mixture into a large bowl. Whisking continuously, gradually pour the hot cream mixture into the bowl with the egg mixture. Skim off any bubbles that form. Divide mixture among four 1-cup (225ml) ramekins or ovenproof dishes; cover tightly with aluminum foil.

3 Carefully pour the 1 cup (250ml) boiling water into the inner pot. Place the wire rack in the pot, then place ramekins on rack. Cover with the pressure-cooker lid; lock the lid, ensuring steam-release valve and quick-release button are up. Select **PRESSURE COOK** low heat and set time for 15 minutes.

4 Taking care, quick-release the pressure. Remove ramekins from the inner pot and place in the fridge for 4 hours to chill.

5 Just before serving, halve and pit cherries. Sprinkle 1 tablespoon of the extra sugar over the surface of each custard. Using a kitchen blowtorch, heat sugar until melted to an even golden brown. Serve topped with cherries and raspberries.

CHAR SIU BEEF BAHN MI

Prep 15 mins   **Sauté** 2 mins   **Pressure Cook** 45 mins   **Makes** 8   Dairy-free   Good to freeze

⅓ cup (125g) char siu sauce
   (see tips)
¼ cup (60ml) rice wine vinegar
2 tbsp Sriracha
1 tbsp lemongrass paste
1 tbsp ginger paste
2 garlic cloves, crushed
2 tsp fish sauce
2 tsp soy sauce
1 tbsp sugar
1 large onion, about 7oz (200g),
   halved, sliced
2¼ lb (1kg) beef chuck
8 soft mini-sandwich buns, about
   11oz (320g) in total
10oz (300g) package Asian-style
   undressed coleslaw mix (see tips)
to serve: potato chips

1 Combine char siu sauce, vinegar, sriracha, lemongrass and ginger pastes, garlic, fish sauce, soy sauce, and sugar in a small bowl.

2 Select **SAUTÉ** high heat and preheat for 5 minutes. When the inner pot is hot, add onion, then top with beef and pour over sauce mixture; **SAUTÉ** for 2 minutes or until mixture boils.

3 Cover with the pressure-cooker lid; lock the lid, ensuring steam-release valve and quick-release button are up. Select **PRESSURE COOK** high heat and set time for 45 minutes.

4 Taking care, quick-release the pressure. Transfer beef to a plate and shred using two forks.

Return shredded meat to the inner pot and stir through sauce to coat.

5 Fill sandwich buns with coleslaw and char siu beef. Serve with potato chips.

TIPS Char siu sauce is available at Asian grocers and larger supermarkets.

To make your own coleslaw mix, combine 1 cup (75g) each of shredded red and green cabbage with 2 thinly sliced spring onions (scallions) and ⅓ cup (10g) torn flat-leaf parsley leaves.

Only the char siu beef is suitable to freeze.

SPICED LENTIL SOUP WITH ZA'ATAR CHICKPEAS

Prep 5 mins **Sauté** 4 mins **Pressure Cook** 12 mins **Air Fry** 12 mins **Serves** 4–6 Vegetarian

2 tbsp extra virgin olive oil

1 large onion, about 7oz (200g), thinly sliced

2 garlic cloves, crushed

½ tsp ground turmeric

3 tsp ground cumin

2 cups (400g) dried red lentils, rinsed, drained

1 medium potato, about 7oz (200g), peeled, coarsely chopped

8 cups (2 liters) vegetable stock

15oz (425g) can chickpeas, drained, rinsed

1 tbsp za'atar

2 tbsp lemon juice

to serve: Greek-style yogurt, extra za'atar, extra virgin olive oil, and toasted flatbread (see tips)

1 Select **SAUTÉ** high heat and preheat for 5 minutes. When the inner pot is hot, add 1 tablespoon of the oil, then add onion; **SAUTÉ**, stirring occasionally, for 3 minutes or until softened slightly. Add garlic, turmeric, and 2 teaspoons of the cumin; **SAUTÉ** for 1 minute or until fragrant. Add lentils, potato, and stock. Turn off **SAUTÉ**.

2 Cover with the pressure-cooker lid; lock the lid, ensuring steam-release valve and quick-release button are up. Select **PRESSURE COOK** high heat and set time for 12 minutes.

3 Combine chickpeas, za'atar, remaining cumin, and remaining oil in a medium bowl; season with salt and pepper. Put half of the chickpea mixture in the air-fryer basket, then place the perforated tray on top. Place remaining chickpeas on the tray. Set aside.

4 Taking care, quick-release the pressure. Using a hand-held or high-speed blender, purée soup until smooth. Stir in lemon juice; season with salt and pepper. Transfer to a heatproof bowl and cover to keep warm.

5 Rinse the inner pot and return to the appliance. Place the air-fryer basket in the inner pot. Cover with the air-fryer lid. Select **AIR FRY** and set temperature to 400°F/200°C and time for 12 minutes; **AIR FRY** until chickpeas are crisp.

6 Divide soup among bowls; top with yogurt, chickpeas, and extra za'atar. Drizzle with extra olive oil. Serve with flatbread.

TIPS Soup will thicken on standing; thin with a little just-boiled water if needed.

Flatbread can be toasted using the air-fryer function.

ASIAN-STYLE PORK BELLY WITH CRACKLING

Prep 10 mins (+ refrigeration)   **Pressure Cook** 25 mins   **Air Fry** 25 mins   **Serves** 4   Dairy-free

1¾ lb (800g) pork belly, skin on
2 tsp Chinese five-spice powder
2½ tsp fine sea salt
2 tbsp soy sauce
2 tbsp Shaohsing rice wine
2 shallots (50g), thickly sliced
2-in (5cm) piece of fresh ginger,
   about 1oz (30g), thinly sliced
5 garlic cloves, bruised
2 tsp sugar
1 star anise
1 tsp baking powder
1 tbsp vegetable oil
1 bunch gai lan or broccolini,
   about 6oz (175g)
to serve: sliced red chile in
   soy sauce

1 Place pork, skin-side down, on a chopping board and rub the flesh only with five-spice. Transfer pork, skin-side up, to a plate. Refrigerate, uncovered, for 2 hours or overnight.

2 Rub 1½ teaspoons of the sea salt into the pork skin. Put soy sauce, rice wine, shallots, ginger, garlic, sugar, star anise, and 1 cup (250ml) water in the inner pot; stir to combine. Place pork, skin-side up, in the pot, ensuring the skin sits above the liquid.

3 Cover with the pressure-cooker lid; lock the lid, ensuring steam-release valve and quick-release button are up. Select **PRESSURE COOK** high heat and set time for 25 minutes.

4 Meanwhile, combine baking powder and remaining salt.

5 Taking care, quick-release the pressure.

Transfer pork, skin-side up, to a chopping board; reserve cooking liquid in a small bowl. Using paper towel, pat pork skin dry. Pierce skin all over with a fork; rub with baking powder mixture, then brush with oil.

6 Place the perforated tray in the air-fryer basket, then place the basket in the inner pot. Place pork on the tray. Cover with the air-fryer lid. Select **AIR FRY** and set temperature to 400°F/200°C and time for 25 minutes; **AIR FRY** until pork is golden and crisp.

7 Put gai lan or broccolini in a bowl and pour over boiling water from the kettle. Blanch for 2 minutes, then drain.

8 Slice pork belly and serve drizzled with warmed reserved cooking liquid and sliced red chile in soy sauce.

AIR FRY

For crisp-fried dishes with less
of the fat, turn to the air-fry function
on your Instant Pot. Cook all your
fast-food favorites and more,
including a tempting cheesecake.

KARAAGE (JAPANESE "FRIED" CHICKEN)

Prep 10 mins (+ refrigeration)   **Air Fry** 24 mins   **Serves** 4   Dairy-free   Gluten-free

1 tsp finely grated fresh ginger, including any ginger juice
2 garlic cloves, crushed
1½ tbsp gluten-free soy sauce
1 tbsp sake
1 tbsp mirin (see tips)
1½ lb (750g) boneless, skinless chicken thighs, trimmed and cut into 2in (5cm) pieces
1 cup (150g) potato starch (see tips)
2 tbsp sesame seeds
oil cooking spray
to serve: Japanese gluten-free mayonnaise (see tips) and shichimi togarashi (see tips)

1 Combine ginger, garlic, soy sauce, sake, and mirin in a large bowl; add chicken and mix until well coated. Cover and refrigerate for 30 minutes to marinate.

2 Meanwhile, combine potato starch and sesame seeds in a bowl. Toss drained chicken in the mixture to coat, shaking off any excess. Spray chicken with oil until well coated.

3 Place the air-fryer basket in the inner pot. Place a quarter of the chicken, evenly spaced, in the basket, then place the perforated tray on top. Place another quarter of the chicken, evenly spaced, on the tray. Cover with the air-fryer lid. Select **AIR FRY** and set temperature to 200°C/400°F and time for 12 minutes; **AIR FRY**, turning halfway through cooking,

until chicken is lightly golden. Repeat with remaining chicken.

4 Serve karaage with Japanese mayonnaise sprinkled with togarashi.

TIPS Most mirin is gluten-free; however, check the label first.

Potato starch is available from Asian grocers and should not be confused with potato flour.

Japanese mayonnaise is made with egg yolks only and has a more velvety texture than other mayonnaises, as well as a rich umami flavor with extra tang.

Shichimi togarashi (Japanese seven-spice mix) is available from larger supermarkets and specialty grocers.

CARAMELIZED ONION & PROSCIUTTO BURGERS

Prep 10 mins **Air Fry** 10 mins **Serves** 4

1½ lb (750g) ground pork and veal (see tips)
1 egg, lightly beaten
½ cup (40g) finely grated Parmesan cheese
¼ cup (70g) onion jam or caramelized onions
¼ cup (25g) sage and onion stuffing mix
8 slices of prosciutto
1 Romaine heart, shredded
4 brioche hamburger buns, split, toasted (see tips)
4 slices of mozzarella
to serve: extra onion jam or caramelized onions and French fries (see tips)

1 Combine ground meat, egg, Parmesan cheese, onions, and stuffing mix in a large bowl; season with salt and pepper. Shape into four patties, then wrap 2 slices of prosciutto around each patty.

2 Place the air-fryer basket in the inner pot. Arrange patties in a single layer in the basket. Cover with the air-fryer lid. Select **AIR FRY** and set temperature to 400°F/200°C and time for 10 minutes; **AIR FRY**, turning halfway through cooking, until patties are browned and cooked through.

3 Place shredded lettuce and a hamburger patty on the bottom half of each brioche bun; top each patty with a slice of mozzarella and extra onion jam or caramelized onions, then sandwich together with brioche lids. Serve burgers with fries.

TIPS Ground pork and veal is a perfect blend of flavor and fattiness. You can also use 100 percent ground beef or lamb, but avoid chicken because it tends to be too lean.

You can **AIR FRY** the brioche buns for 4 minutes to toast. You can also **AIR FRY** the fries following package directions.

POTATO, SALMON & DILL CROQUETTES

Prep 10 mins   **Air Fry** 28 mins   **Makes** 16   Good to freeze   Pescatarian

16oz (453g) ready-to-eat
   mashed potatoes
10oz (300g) hot-smoked salmon,
   skin removed, flaked
3 spring onions (scallions),
   thinly sliced
½ cup (60g) grated Cheddar
3 eggs
1 tbsp Dijon mustard
1½ cups (150g) sage and onion
   stuffing mix, finely crushed
2 tbsp finely chopped dill (see tip)
2 tbsp finely chopped flat-leaf
   parsley (see tip)
olive oil cooking spray
to serve: extra dill sprigs (optional),
   lemon aïoli or mayonnaise
   swirled with harissa paste,
   lemon wedges

1 Place mashed potatoes in a medium bowl and stir until smooth. Add salmon, spring onions, Cheddar, one of the eggs, mustard, ½ cup (50g) of the stuffing mix, and the dill; stir to combine. Season to taste with salt and pepper.
2 Whisk remaining eggs in a shallow bowl. Place remaining stuffing mix and the parsley in another shallow bowl.
3 Shape potato mixture into 3 x 1in (7 x 3cm) ovals. Working with one at a time, dip in egg, then coat in stuffing and parsley mix.
4 Place the air-fryer basket in the inner pot. Spray croquettes with oil to coat well. Arrange half of the croquettes in a single layer in the air-fryer basket. Cover with the air-fryer lid. Select **AIR FRY** and set temperature to 400°F/200°C and time for 14 minutes; **AIR FRY**, turning halfway through cooking, until croquettes are golden. Repeat with remaining croquettes.
5 Scatter croquettes with extra dill sprigs, if you like. Serve with lemon aïoli swirled with a little harissa, and lemon wedges for squeezing over.

TIP You can omit the dill and double the quantity of parsley used, if you like.

LEMON & BLUEBERRY CHEESECAKE

Prep 10 mins (+ cooling & refrigeration)   **Air Fry** 30 mins   **Sauté** 8 mins
Serves 8   Good to freeze

---

5 tbsp (70g) unsalted butter, melted

1 cup (128g) graham cracker crumbs

3 x 8oz (226g) packages cream cheese, at room temperature

3 eggs

14oz (396g) can sweetened condensed milk

2 tsp finely grated lemon zest

½ tsp sea salt flakes

2 cups (300g) frozen blueberries, thawed

2 tbsp lemon juice

⅓ cup (75g) sugar

1 Grease a 7in (18cm) springform cake pan with a little of the melted butter; line the bottom of the pan with parchment paper.

2 In a food processor, combine graham cracker crumbs and add remaining melted butter and process until combined. Press mixture over the bottom of the pan. Allow to freeze for 10 minutes.

3 Using an electric mixer, beat cream cheese in a large bowl for 2 minutes or until smooth. Add eggs one at a time, beating well after each addition. Add condensed milk, lemon zest, and salt; beat for 2 minutes or until creamy and smooth. Transfer mixture to a bowl.

4 Place the air-fryer base in the inner pot. Lower pan into the pot. Carefully pour cheesecake mixture into the pan. Cover with the air-fryer lid. Select **AIR FRY** and set temperature to 300°F/150°C and time for 30 minutes; **AIR FRY** until cheesecake is firm around the edge with a slight wobble in the center. Remove the air-fryer lid. Cool in the inner pot at room temperature for 1 hour, then transfer pan to the fridge for at least 6 hours to chill.

5 To make the syrup, put blueberries, lemon juice, and sugar in the inner pot. Select **SAUTÉ** high heat; **SAUTÉ** for 8 minutes until syrup is slightly thickened. Transfer to a serving bowl and refrigerate until needed.

6 Release cheesecake from the pan and transfer to a serving plate. Serve with blueberry syrup drizzled over the top.

TIP If you can't find graham cracker crumbs, crush graham crackers in the food processor, or in a bag with a rolling pin.

99

CRISP GNOCCHI WITH CREAMY PESTO DIPPING SAUCE

Prep 10 mins   **Pressure cook** 1 min   **Air Fry** 15 mins   **Serves** 6   Vegetarian

1 lb (450g) ready-made potato gnocchi (see tip)
1 tbsp extra virgin olive oil
1 tsp garlic salt
to serve: sea salt flakes and basil leaves (optional)

CREAMY PESTO DIPPING SAUCE
½ cup (25g) firmly packed basil leaves
2 tbsp pine nuts, toasted
2 tbsp finely grated Parmesan-style vegetarian cheese
1 garlic clove, crushed
⅓ cup (80g) sour cream

1 Fill the inner pot with 1½ cups (375ml) water, then add gnocchi. Cover with the pressure-cooker lid; lock the lid, ensuring steam-release valve and quick-release button are up. Select **PRESSURE COOK** high heat and set time for 1 minute. Naturally release the pressure for 3 minutes, then, taking care, quick-release the pressure; this will result in perfectly cooked gnocchi. Again taking care, drain gnocchi well. Spread gnocchi over a tray to air-dry. Dry the inner pot and return to the appliance. Place the air-fryer basket in the inner pot.

2 To make the creamy pesto dipping sauce, combine basil, pine nuts, Parmesan cheese, and garlic in a small food processor until finely chopped. Add sour cream and process until smooth. Season to taste with salt and pepper.

3 Put gnocchi, oil, and garlic salt in a large bowl; toss to coat gnocchi in the oil mixture.

4 Place gnocchi in the air-fryer basket. Cover with the air-fryer lid. Select **AIR FRY** and set temperature to 400°F/200°C and time for 15 minutes; **AIR FRY**, stirring occasionally, until gnocchi is golden.

5 Sprinkle crisp gnocchi with sea salt flakes and scatter with basil leaves. Serve with the creamy pesto dipping sauce.

TIP Substitute potato gnocchi with pumpkin or beetroot gnocchi, if you like.

CORN CHIP-COATED CHICKEN WITH RANCH SAUCE

Prep 10 mins   **Air Fry** 15 mins   **Serves** 4   Good to freeze

8oz (225g) corn chips
1 tsp dried oregano
1 tsp smoked paprika
1 tsp sea salt flakes
½ tsp mustard powder
¼ cup (35g) flour
2 eggs
2½ lb (1.2kg) chicken tenderloins
olive oil cooking spray

RANCH SAUCE
½ cup (120g) sour cream
½ cup (150g) mayonnaise
½ cup (125ml) buttermilk
¼ cup (15g) finely chopped dill
1 spring onion (scallion), finely sliced
1 tbsp lemon juice

1 Put corn chips in a large zip-top sandwich bag and seal. Use your hands or a rolling pin to crush the corn chips, then transfer to a shallow bowl and stir in oregano, paprika, sea salt flakes, and mustard powder. Place flour in a second shallow bowl. Lightly beat eggs in a third shallow bowl. Dust chicken in flour, shaking off any excess, then dip in egg and coat in corn chips. Spray generously all over with oil.
2 Place the air-fryer basket in the inner pot. Cover with the air-fryer lid. Select **AIR FRY** and set temperature to 350°F/180°C and time for 3 minutes to preheat.
3 To make the ranch sauce, combine ingredients in a medium bowl. Transfer to a serving bowl.

4 Spray the air-fryer basket with oil. Place half of the coated chicken in the basket, then place the perforated tray on top and spray with oil. Place remaining coated chicken on the tray. Cover with the air-fryer lid. Select **AIR FRY** and set temperature to 350°F/180°C and time for 15 minutes; **AIR FRY**, turning halfway through cooking, until chicken is golden and cooked through.
5 Serve corn chip-coated chicken with ranch sauce.

TIP You could also serve the chicken with mayonnaise swirled with Sriracha sauce.

103

CHURROS SHELLS WITH CHOCOLATE SAUCE

Prep 5 mins   **Pressure Cook** 2 mins   **Sauté** 8 mins   **Air Fry** 9 mins   **Serves** 4

8oz (225g) large pasta shells
4oz (125g) dark chocolate, chopped
½ cup (125ml) heavy cream
olive oil cooking spray
3 tbsp (40g) butter, melted
⅓ cup (75g) sugar
1 tsp ground cinnamon

1 Fill the inner pot with 2 cups (500ml) water, then add the pasta. Cover with the pressure-cooker lid; lock the lid, ensuring steam-release valve and quick-release button are up. Select **PRESSURE COOK** high heat and set time for 2 minutes. Naturally release the pressure for 3 minutes, then, taking care, quick-release the pressure; this will result in perfectly cooked pasta. Again taking care, drain pasta well. Spread over a clean kitchen towel to air-dry. Dry the inner pot and return to the appliance.

2 Meanwhile, to make the chocolate sauce, put chocolate and cream in a small heatproof bowl, then place bowl in the inner pot. Select **SAUTÉ** low heat and set time for 8 minutes; **SAUTÉ**, stirring occasionally, until the sauce is smooth and combined. Carefully remove the bowl from the inner pot and cover to keep warm. Wash the inner pot and return to the appliance.

3 Spray the air-fryer basket with oil and place in the inner pot. Put pasta in a bowl and toss with melted butter to coat. Add pasta to the air-fryer basket. Cover with the air-fryer lid. Select **AIR FRY** and set temperature to 400°F/200°C and time for 9 minutes; **AIR FRY**, stirring, until pasta is golden.

4 Meanwhile, to make the cinnamon sugar, combine sugar and cinnamon in a shallow bowl. Immediately tip hot pasta into cinnamon sugar and toss to coat.

5 Serve churros shells with warm chocolate sauce.

FURIKAKE ASPARAGUS

Prep 10 mins   **Air Fry** 4 mins   **Serves** 4 (as a snack)   Dairy-free   Vegetarian

1 cup (75g) panko breadcrumbs
¼ cup (30g) furikake (see tip)
1 tbsp sesame oil
2 eggs
12oz (340g) thick asparagus
    spears, trimmed
olive oil cooking spray
1 tsp wasabi powder
⅓ cup (100g) Japanese mayonnaise
    (see tips on page 93)
to serve: extra furikake and
    lemon sides

1 Put breadcrumbs, furikake, and sesame oil in a medium bowl; stir to combine. Transfer breadcrumb mixture to a tray. Using a fork, lightly beat eggs in a shallow bowl; season with salt and pepper.

2 Place the air-fryer basket in the inner pot. Cover with the air-fryer lid. Select **AIR FRY** and set temperature to 350°F/180°C and time for 3 minutes to preheat.

3 Dip asparagus in egg, shaking off any excess, then roll in breadcrumb mixture. Place on a baking tray and spray generously with oil to coat all sides.

4 Spray the air-fryer basket with oil. Put half of the coated asparagus in the basket, then place the perforated tray on top and spray with oil.

Place remaining coated asparagus on the tray. Cover with the air-fryer lid. Select **AIR FRY** and again set temperature to 350°F/180°C and time for 4 minutes; **AIR FRY** until asparagus is golden.

5 Meanwhile, combine wasabi powder and Japanese mayonnaise in a small bowl.

6 Sprinkle asparagus with extra furikake seasoning. Serve with wasabi mayonnaise and lemon cheeks for squeezing over.

TIP A Japanese rice seasoning, furikake usually contains toasted sesame seeds, salt, nori, and sugar. It may also include bonito flakes, chile flakes, miso powder, shiitake powder, and poppy seeds. Look for it at Japanese and specialty grocers.

ROAST

Goodbye oven, hello versatile Instant Pot. Switch on the roast function, and you will soon be enjoying crisp-skinned chicken and fish, succulent roasts, caramelized veggies, and Spanish-style tortas.

MALAYSIAN NYONYA CURRY ROAST CHICKEN

Prep 10 mins   **Sauté** 7 mins   **Roast** 55 mins   **Serves** 4   Dairy-free   Gluten-free

4 anchovies, finely chopped
6½ oz (185g) jar Nyonya curry paste
3¼ lb (1.5kg) whole chicken
2 tbsp olive oil
1¾ lb (800g) new or baby potatoes, unpeeled
¾ lb (400g) carrots, trimmed, peeled, halved
8oz (225g) green beans, trimmed
13.5oz (400ml) can coconut milk
to serve: cilantro sprigs, steamed rice, and lime halves

1 Combine anchovies and curry paste in a bowl; reserve ¼ cup (60ml) for the sauce. Rub remaining paste mixture all over chicken and under the skin of the breast meat. Tuck the wings under and tie chicken legs together with kitchen string.

2 Add half of the oil and the potatoes to the inner pot; toss to coat. Add chicken to the pot. Cover with the air-fryer lid. Select **ROAST** and set temperature to 375°F/190°C and time for 40 minutes; **ROAST** until chicken is cooked through. Transfer to a plate, partially cover, and allow to rest for 15 minutes.

3 Meanwhile, add carrots and ¼ cup (60ml) water to the inner pot (there is no need to clean it). Cover with the air-fryer lid. Select **ROAST** and set temperature to 375°F/190°C and time

for 10 minutes; **ROAST** until carrots are almost tender.

4 Add green beans to the inner pot. Re-cover with the air-fryer lid. Select **ROAST** and set temperature to 375°F/190°C and time for 5 minutes; **ROAST** until vegetables are tender. Using a slotted spoon, transfer vegetables to a plate and keep warm. Drain the inner pot, dry, and return to the appliance.

5 To make the curry sauce, select **SAUTÉ** high heat and preheat for 5 minutes. When the inner pot is hot, add remaining oil and reserved curry paste; **SAUTÉ** for 2 minutes. Stir in coconut milk and bring to a simmer; **SAUTÉ** for 5 minutes until slightly reduced.

6 Serve roast chicken with vegetables, cilantro sprigs, curry sauce, rice, and lime cheeks for squeezing over.

CHINESE-STYLE ROAST LAMB

Prep 15 mins (+ refrigeration & resting)   **Roast** 45 mins   **Serves** 4   Dairy-free

1 small red onion, about 3½oz
   (100g), coarsely chopped
4 garlic cloves, peeled
1½ in (4cm) piece of fresh ginger,
   coarsely chopped
1 long red chile, coarsely chopped
¾ cup (35g) coarsely chopped
   cilantro stems, roots, and leaves
1 tbsp ground cumin
1 tbsp ground coriander
½ tsp ground white pepper
2 tbsp sesame oil
2 tbsp rice wine vinegar
¼ cup (60ml) soy sauce
4 lb (1.8kg) boneless lamb leg,
   trimmed, halved
to serve: steamed bok choy or
   broccolini and steamed rice

1 Process onion, garlic, ginger, chile, cilantro, spices, pepper, sesame oil, vinegar, and soy sauce in a food processor or blender until almost smooth. Place lamb in a large dish and pour over spice mixture to coat; cover and refrigerate for 3 hours or overnight.

2 Place the wire rack in the inner pot. Place lamb on the rack and pour over any marinade. Cover with the air-fryer lid. Select **ROAST** and set temperature to 400°F/200°C and time for 45 minutes; **ROAST** until lamb is cooked through.

3 Remove the air-fryer lid. Partially cover the lamb and allow to rest for 10 minutes in the inner pot. Slice lamb and serve drizzled with cooking juices, with bok choy or broccolini and steamed rice.

ONE-POT SALMON NIÇOISE BAKE

Prep 10 mins   **Roast** 39 mins   **Serves** 4   Dairy-free   Gluten-free   Pescatarian

1lb (450g) fingerling potatoes, halved lengthwise

1 medium garlic bulb, cloves separated

¼ cup (60ml) extra virgin olive oil

4 whole eggs, shells washed

8oz (225g) cherry tomatoes on the vine

½ cup (80g) pitted Kalamata olives

1¼lb (600g) boneless salmon fillets, skin on

8oz (225g) green beans, trimmed

SALSA VERDE

½ cup (12g) firmly packed flat-leaf parsley

½ cup (30g) firmly packed baby spinach leaves

4 anchovy fillets

2 tbsp capers

2 tbsp lemon juice

½ cup (125ml) extra virgin olive oil

1 Put potatoes and garlic in the inner pot; drizzle with 1 tablespoon of the oil; season with salt and pepper. Place the wire rack in the inner pot, then place eggs on top. Cover with the air-fryer lid. Select **ROAST** and set temperature to 400°F/200°C and time for 10 minutes; **ROAST**, stirring potatoes halfway through cooking and turning eggs.

2 Remove eggs and plunge into a bowl of ice-cold water, then peel and set aside. Cover pot again with the air-fryer lid. Select **ROAST** and set temperature to 400°F/200°C and time for 15 minutes; **ROAST** until potatoes and garlic are golden. Transfer potatoes and garlic to a plate and cover to keep warm.

3 Add cherry tomatoes and olives to the inner pot; drizzle with remaining oil. Cover with the air-fryer lid. Select **ROAST** and set

temperature to 400°F/200°C and time for 10 minutes.

4 Push tomato mixture to one side of the inner pot. Add seasoned salmon to the other side, skin-side down, ensuring salmon sits directly on the bottom of the pot. Cover again with the air-fryer lid. Select **ROAST** and set temperature to 400°F/200°C and time for 2 minutes. Turn salmon over and add green beans; **ROAST** at 400°F/200°C for a further 2 minutes or until salmon is just cooked through and green beans are tender.

5 Meanwhile, to make the salsa verde, process ingredients in a small food processor until combined.

6 Arrange salmon, potatoes, garlic, cherry tomatoes, green beans, olives, and halved eggs on a platter or plates. Serve with salsa verde.

CHORIZO & SUN-DRIED TOMATO TORTA

Prep 15 mins   **Sauté** 5 mins   **Pressure cook** 1 min   **Roast** 1 hr   **Serves** 6   Good to freeze

1¼ lb (600g) Russet potatoes, peeled, cut into ¼in (5mm)-thick slices

2 tbsp extra virgin olive oil

1 large onion, about 7oz (200g), thinly sliced

2 garlic cloves, crushed

8oz (225g) cured chorizo sausages, thinly sliced

¾ cup (135g) sun-dried tomatoes, coarsely chopped

2 medium zucchini, about 9oz (240g) in total, coarsely grated, squeezed dry

10 eggs, lightly beaten

1 cup (120g) coarsely grated Cheddar

2 cups (35g) red-veined sorrel or arugula leaves

1 tbsp balsamic vinegar

⅓ cup (25g) shaved Parmesan cheese

1 Put potatoes and 1½ cups (375ml) water in the inner pot. Select **PRESSURE COOK** high heat and set time for 1 minute. Taking care, quick-release the pressure. Drain potato slices, then spread out on a tray to cool. Dry the inner pot and return to the appliance.

2 Select **SAUTÉ** high heat and preheat for 5 minutes. Add 1 tablespoon of the oil. When oil is hot, add onion, garlic. and chorizo; **SAUTÉ**, stirring, for 5 minutes. Stir in sun-dried tomatoes and zucchini; season to taste.

3 Grease a deep 8in (20cm) round cake pan; line with parchment paper. Combine egg and half of the Cheddar; season with salt and pepper. Cover the bottom of the pan with potato slices, then pour over half of the egg mixture. Spread chorizo mixture evenly over potatoes. Pour remaining egg mixture over chorizo mixture, then scatter with remaining Cheddar. Cover pan with aluminum foil.

4 Place the wire rack in the inner pot, then carefully place the pan on top. Cover with the air-fryer lid. Select **ROAST** and set temperature to 400°F/200°C and time for 50 minutes.

5 Remove the aluminum foil, then cover again with the air-fryer lid. Select **ROAST** and set temperature to 400°F/200°C and time for 10 minutes; **ROAST** until top of the torta is golden.

6 Toss greens with oil, the vinegar, and Parmesan cheese; season to taste with salt and pepper. Serve torta with salad.

TAMARIND PORK BELLY

Prep 10 mins (+ resting)   **Roast** 30 mins   **Serves** 4   Good to freeze

4 garlic cloves, crushed
2 tbsp finely grated fresh ginger
6 spring onions (scallions),
    finely chopped
1 long red chile, seeded,
    finely chopped
1½ tbsp tamarind paste
1 tbsp toasted sesame oil
¼ cup (60ml) soy sauce
1½ tbsp fish sauce
2½ tbsp light soft brown sugar
2¼ lb (1kg) pork belly, skin removed
½ chicken bouillon cube
1 tbsp lime juice
to serve: shredded green cabbage

1 Combine garlic, ginger, spring onions, chile, tamarind paste, sesame oil, soy sauce, fish sauce, and sugar in a large bowl; add pork and toss to coat.
2 Remove pork from the marinade. Pour marinade into the inner pot; crumble the bouillon cube into the mixture. Place the wire rack in the inner pot, then place pork on top. Cover with the air-fryer lid. Select **ROAST** and set temperature to 400°F/200°C and time for 30 minutes; **ROAST** until pork is tender and cooked through.

3 Remove the air-fryer lid. Partially cover the pork and allow to rest for 10 minutes in the inner pot before slicing. Stir lime juice into the sauce in the pot until evenly mixed.
4 Serve pork belly slices drizzled with a little of the sauce, with remaining sauce and shredded cabbage on the side.

MISO CHICKPEA LOADED SWEET POTATOES

Prep 10 mins   **Sauté** 10 mins   **Roast** 35 mins   **Serves** 4   Vegetarian

2 tbsp extra virgin olive oil

2 large red onions, about 1lb 5oz (600g) in total, each cut into 8 wedges

4 garlic cloves, thinly sliced

2 long red chiles, halved lengthwise

1 tbsp finely grated fresh ginger

1 cup (250ml) salt-reduced vegetable stock

1½ tbsp tamari

1½ tbsp maple syrup

1 tbsp lemon juice

2½ tbsp red miso paste (aka miso) (see tip)

2 x 15oz (425g) cans chickpeas, drained, rinsed

2¼ lb (1kg) sweet potatoes

3 tbsp (40g) butter

2 spring onions (scallions), shredded

¼ cup (7g) cilantro leaves

1 Select **SAUTÉ** high heat and preheat for 5 minutes. When the inner pot is hot, add oil, then add onion; **SAUTÉ**, stirring, for 5 minutes or until onion is softened. Add garlic, chiles, and ginger; **SAUTÉ**, stirring, for a further 2 minutes.

2 Whisk stock, tamari, maple syrup, lemon juice, and miso in a small bowl; add to the inner pot. Select **SAUTÉ** high heat and bring to a boil, then boil for 1 minute. Stir in chickpeas.

3 Prick sweet potatoes several times with a fork and place on top of chickpea mixture. Cover with the air-fryer lid. Select **ROAST** and set temperature to 400°F/200°C and time for 35 minutes; **ROAST** until sweet potatoes are tender.

Transfer sweet potatoes to plates. With a small, sharp knife, slit top of sweet potatoes lengthwise to open them up.

4 Gently stir butter into chickpea mixture in the inner pot until combined.

5 Fill sweet potatoes with chickpea mixture. Serve topped with spring onions and cilantro.

TIP Red miso (aka miso) is fermented for longer than other types of miso, and is generally saltier than milder-flavored white miso (shiro miso). It is available from most major supermarkets and Asian grocers.

MISO-ROASTED CAULIFLOWER WITH ALMOND CREAM

Prep 15 mins   **Roast** 40 mins   **Serves** 4   Dairy-free   Vegetarian

2½ lb (1.2kg) head of cauliflower, outer leaves and stem trimmed
2 tbsp white miso (shiro miso) paste (see tips)
2 tbsp gochujang (Korean chili paste) (see tips)
¼ cup (60ml) maple syrup
2 tbsp extra virgin olive oil
1 tbsp finely grated fresh ginger
2 garlic cloves, crushed
1 cup (250ml) Shaohsing rice wine
1 tbsp sesame seeds

ALMOND CREAM
1¼ cups (200g) flaked almonds
¼ cup (75g) Japanese mayonnaise (see tips on page 93)
1½ tbsp white miso (shiro miso) paste
2 tbsp yuzu juice or lemon juice (see tips)

1 Cut a cross in the base of the cauliflower with a sharp knife. Combine miso, gochujang, maple syrup, oil, ginger, and garlic in a small bowl; season with salt if needed. Spread mixture over cauliflower. Pour rice wine into the inner pot, then place cauliflower in the pot.
2 Cover the inner pot with aluminum foil, then cover with the air-fryer lid. Select **ROAST** and set temperature to 400°F/200°C and time for 25 minutes.
3 Remove the aluminum foil, sprinkle cauliflower with sesame seeds, then cover again with the air-fryer lid. Select **ROAST** and set temperature to 400°F/200°C and time for 15 minutes; **ROAST** until cauliflower is tender.
4 Meanwhile, to make the almond cream, place almonds in a heatproof bowl and cover with boiling water. Allow to stand until cooled, then drain. Blend soaked almonds with remaining ingredients and ¾ cup (185ml) water until smooth.
5 Serve roasted cauliflower with almond cream.

TIPS Shiro (white) miso is sweeter and milder in taste than brown, red, and black miso. It is available from most major supermarkets and Asian grocers.

Gochujang is a spicy Korean red chili paste available from larger supermarkets and Asian grocers.

Yuzu, a popular Japanese citrus fruit, has a zesty flavor with a strong aromatic perfume. Yuzu juice can be found at Asian and specialty grocers.

KOREAN ROAST BEEF WITH BRAISED CABBAGE

Prep 10 mins (+ refrigeration)   **Roast** 1 hr 45 mins   **Sauté** 7 mins   **Serves** 4   Dairy-free

¼ cup (75g) gochujang (Korean chili paste) (see tip)
3 garlic cloves, crushed
1½ in (4cm) piece of fresh ginger about 1oz (30g), finely grated
1 tbsp light soft brown sugar
2 tsp sesame oil
2¼ lb (1kg) beef chuck roast
1 small Napa or Savoy cabbage, about 1½ lb (700g), coarsely chopped
2 spring onions (scallions), cut into 2-in (5cm) lengths
2 tsp fish sauce
1 cup (250ml) beef stock
to serve: steamed rice

1 Combine gochujang, garlic, ginger, brown sugar, and sesame oil in a small bowl; reserve 1 tablespoon of the marinade for later use. Place beef in a large dish and rub with the marinade; cover and refrigerate for at least 4 hours or overnight.

2 Place the wire rack in the inner pot, then place beef on top. Cover with the air-fryer lid. Select **ROAST** and set temperature to 375°F/190°C and time for 20 minutes; **ROAST** until beef is lightly charred.

3 Cover beef with aluminum foil, then cover again with the air-fryer lid. Select **ROAST** and set temperature to 375°F/190°C and time for 1 hour 25 minutes; **ROAST**, turning halfway through cooking, until beef is medium-rare or cooked to your liking. Transfer beef to a plate and allow to rest for 15 minutes.

4 Pour beef fat from the inner pot into a small bowl and reserve. Clean the inner pot and return to the appliance. Add reserved fat to the pot, then add Napa or Savoy cabbage and spring onions. Select **SAUTÉ** high heat and set time for 2 minutes; **SAUTÉ** until vegetables are softened. Add fish sauce, stock, and reserved marinade; **SAUTÉ** for a further 5 minutes. Season to taste with salt and pepper.

5 Slice beef and serve with vegetables and rice.

CHICKEN & CORN WITH SAGE & CAPER BUTTER

Prep 20 mins   **Roast** 35 mins   **Sauté** 15 mins   **Serves** 4

3¼ lb (1.2kg) Maryland-cut chicken (including drumstick and thigh), skin on

2 cups (500ml) chicken stock

1 medium lemon, about 5oz (140g), sliced

4 garlic cloves, bruised

2 tbsp chopped sage leaves

4 cobs of corn, about 15oz (425g) in total, husks and silk removed, broken into pieces

SAGE & CAPER BUTTER

½ cup (125g) butter, softened

2 garlic cloves, crushed

2 tsp finely grated lemon zest

1 tbsp finely chopped sage

1 tbsp capers, chopped

1 To make the sage and caper butter, combine ingredients in a bowl.

2 Pat chicken dry with paper towels. Run a couple of fingers between the flesh and skin to separate, then spread the sage butter between flesh and skin. Season with salt.

3 Put stock, lemon, garlic, sage, and corn in the inner pot. Place the wire rack in the inner pot, then place chicken in a single layer on top. Cover with the air-fryer lid. Select **ROAST** and set temperature to 400°F/200°C and time for 35 minutes; **ROAST** until chicken is crisp and cooked through. Transfer chicken to a plate and partially cover to keep warm.

4 Select **SAUTÉ** high heat and set time for 15 minutes; **SAUTÉ** until cooking liquid is reduced and thickened.

5 Serve chicken and corn drizzled with reduced cooking liquid.

TIP Turn chicken halfway through the cooking time for even browning.

DEHYDRATE

Use the air-fryer lid and dehydrate function for low-temperature cooking. You will be creating tasty snacks and treats, as well as citrus powders for flavorings and seasonings, in no time at all.

SPICY DRIED MANGO

We recommend you use a 5-tier dehydrator rack to maximize the space of your appliance (see tip).

Prep 5 mins   **Dehydrate** 9 hrs   **Serves** 6   Dairy-free   Gluten-free   Vegetarian

½ tsp chili powder, or to taste
3 medium limes, about 7oz (195g) in total, zest finely grated
¼ tsp fine salt
5 x 15oz (425g) cans mango slices in syrup, drained

1 Combine chili powder, lime zest, and salt in a large bowl.

2 Pat mango slices dry with paper towels, then add to bowl with chili mixture and toss to coat.

3 Arrange mango slices in a single layer on a 5-tier dehydrator rack, then place in the inner pot. Cover with the air-fryer lid. Select **DEHYDRATE** and set temperature to 135°F/57°C and time for 9 hours; **DEHYDRATE** until mango is dried but still retaining a little chewiness.

4 Remove the dehydrator rack from the inner pot. Leave mango slices to cool on the rack. Store in an airtight container for up to 3 months.

TIP If you do not have a 5-tier dehydrator rack, halve the recipe and, in step 3, place half of the mango slices in a single layer in the air-fryer basket; cover with the perforated tray, then arrange remaining mango slices on top. Place the air-fryer basket in the inner pot and continue with the recipe as given.

CITRUS POWDERS

We recommend you use a 5-tier dehydrator rack to maximize the space of your appliance (see tips).

Prep 10 mins   **Dehydrate** 3½–4 hrs   **Makes** 1½–3 tbsp   Dairy-free   Gluten-free   Vegetarian

4 medium limes, about 9oz (260g) in total, each cut into 6 wedges

3 medium lemons, about 15oz (420g) in total, each cut into 6 wedges

2 medium tangelos, about 8oz (225g) in total, each cut into 6 wedges

1 Using a spoon, scoop the flesh from the citrus fruits. Holding a small, sharp knife horizontally, remove the white pith from each citrus wedge and discard.

2 Place citrus rinds in a single layer on a 5-tier dehydrator rack, with the lime rinds on the top two tiers, then place in the inner pot. Cover with the air-fryer lid. Select **DEHYDRATE** and set temperature to 135°F/57°C and time for 3½ hours; **DEHYDRATE** until lime rinds are no longer flexible.

3 Remove the dehydrator rack and transfer lime rinds to a plate. Return dehydrator rack to the inner pot. Cover again with the air-fryer lid. Select **DEHYDRATE** and set temperature to 135°F/57°C and time for 30 minutes; **DEHYDRATE** until lemon and tangelo rinds are no longer flexible.

4 Remove the dehydrator rack from the inner pot. Allow citrus rinds to cool on the rack.

5 Process each citrus rind separately in a high-speed blender to a powder. Store in an airtight container for up to 3 months.

TIPS If you do not have a 5-tier dehydrator rack, make a single citrus powder type rather than all three. Place half of the rinds in a single layer in the air-fryer basket, cover with the perforated tray, then place remaining citrus rinds on the tray. Place the air-fryer basket in the inner pot and continue with the recipe.

Use half as much citrus powder as stipulated for freshly grated zest in cake batters, buttercreams, or mixed with sugar for dusting, to add a citrus flavor.

BEEF JERKY

We recommend you use a 5-tier dehydrator rack to maximize the space of your appliance (see tips).

Prep 10 mins (+ freezing & refrigeration)   **Dehydrate** 8 hrs   **Serves** 8   Dairy-free

1½ lb (800g) flank or skirt steak
½ cup (125ml) soy sauce
½ cup (125ml) Worcestershire sauce
2 tsp freshly ground black pepper
1 tsp sea salt flakes
1 tsp onion powder
1 tsp garlic powder
1 tsp liquid smoke (see tips)

1 Trim excess fat from steak, then place in the freezer for 30 minutes to firm up; this will make it easier to slice. Remove steak from the freezer and thinly slice against the grain into long strips.

2 Whisk remaining ingredients in a small bowl to combine. Place beef and marinade in a large zip-top bag; seal and shake to coat the beef. Refrigerate for 2 hours or overnight.

3 Drain meat. Arrange meat slices in a single layer on a 5-tier dehydrator rack, then place in the inner pot. Cover with the air-fryer lid. Select **DEHYDRATE** and set temperature to 145°F/62°C and time for 8 hours; **DEHYDRATE** until meat is dried.

4 Remove the dehydrator rack from the inner pot. Leave meat to cool on the rack. Store in an airtight container for up to 3 months.

TIPS If you do not have a 5-tier dehydrator rack, halve the recipe and arrange half of the beef in a single layer in the air-fryer basket, cover with the perforated tray, then place remaining beef on top. Place the air-fryer basket in the inner pot and continue with the recipe.

Liquid smoke imparts an instant smoky flavor and aroma to food. It can be found at larger supermarkets, specialty grocers, and select delicatessens. Alternatively, add 2 teaspoons smoked paprika to the marinade instead.

CAULIFLOWER POPCORN

We recommend you use a 5-tier dehydrator rack to maximize the space of your appliance (see tip).

Prep 15 mins   **Dehydrate** 8 hrs   **Serves** 4   Dairy-free   Gluten-free   Vegetarian

⅓ cup (95g) gluten-free hot sauce
¼ cup (60ml) olive oil
2 tsp garlic powder
2 tsp onion powder
1 tbsp smoked paprika
2 tsp ground cumin
2¼ lb (1kg) head of cauliflower, cut into 1-in (2cm) florets
olive oil cooking spray

1 Combine hot sauce, oil, garlic powder, onion powder, paprika, and cumin in a medium bowl; add cauliflower and toss to coat well.

2 Spray a 5-tier dehydrator rack with oil. Arrange cauliflower on the bottom, middle, and top racks, then place in the inner pot. Cover with the air-fryer lid. Select **DEHYDRATE** and set temperature to 165°F/74°C and time for 8 hours; **DEHYDRATE** until cauliflower is dried.

3 Remove the dehydrator rack from the inner pot. Leave cauliflower to cool on the rack. Store in an airtight container for up to 1 month.

TIP If you do not have a 5-tier dehydrator rack, halve the recipe and arrange half of the cauliflower in a single layer in the air-fryer basket, cover with the perforated tray, then place remaining cauliflower on top. Place the air-fryer basket in the inner pot and continue with the recipe.

BAKE

Keep the kitchen cool and
use your Instant Pot instead of
the oven. Whip up an assortment
of baked goods from cakes and
pies to rolls and breads, or a
comforting savory baked dish.

POTATO & FRENCH ONION BAKE

Prep 25 mins   **Bake** 2 hrs 30 mins   **Serves** 4   Vegetarian

2¾ lb (1.2kg) red-skinned
  potatoes, peeled, cut into
  ¼ in (5mm)-thick slices
2 tbsp lemon thyme leaves
1.4oz (40g) package French onion
  soup mix
1¼ cup (300ml) heavy cream
¼ cup (60ml) milk
½ cup (40g) finely grated Parmesan-
  style vegetarian cheese
to serve: extra lemon thyme leaves

1 Lightly grease an 8in (20cm) round cake pan. Arrange potatoes upright in stacks of slices around the edge of the pan, then work towards the center to completely cover the bottom of the pan, scattering with thyme.
2 Combine soup mix, cream, milk, and Parmesan cheese in a large bowl; season with salt and pepper. Pour mixture evenly over the potatoes and allow it to settle. Cover the pan with aluminum foil. Place the pan in the inner pot. Cover with the air-fryer lid. Select **BAKE** and set temperature to 350°F/180°C and time for 2 hours.

3 Remove the aluminum foil, then cover again with the air-fryer lid. Select **BAKE** and set temperature to 400°F/200°C and time for 30 minutes; **BAKE** until potatoes are tender and the top is golden.
4 Allow to stand for 10 minutes before serving. Serve topped with extra thyme leaves.

TIPS Fold two lengths of aluminum foil into long strips and cross under the base of the pan to act as a sling; this will make it easier to lower and lift the pan into and out of the inner pot.

CHELSEA BUNS

Prep 30 mins (+ standing)   **Bake** 30 mins   **Makes** 9   Good to freeze

---

¾ cup (180ml) milk, heated to
   lukewarm, plus about 3 tsp extra,
   to glaze
¼ cup (55g) firmly packed light
   soft brown sugar
2¼ tsp (7g) or 1 packet dried yeast
4 tbsp (50g) butter, melted and
   cooled, plus 2 tbsp (25g) extra,
   softened
3 cups (480g) bread flour
1 tsp cinnamon
¼ tsp allspice
¼ tsp nutmeg
1 egg, lightly beaten
¾ cup (100g) dried cranberries,
   coarsely chopped
½ cup (80g) powdered sugar

TIP You can also use
the appliance to proof the
dough in steps 2 and 3.
To do this, place a folded
kitchen towel in the bottom
of the inner pot, then place
the bowl/cake pan on top.
Select **WARM** and set for
the specified time.

1 Combine the ¾ cup
(180ml) lukewarm milk,
1 tablespoon of the brown
sugar, and the yeast in a
medium bowl. Allow to
stand in a warm place for
10 minutes until mixture is
frothy. Stir in melted butter.
2 Put flour and ½ teaspoon
of cinnamon in the large
bowl of an electric mixer
fitted with a dough hook.
Add yeast mixture and egg;
mix for 10 minutes or until
a smooth, elastic dough
forms. Transfer to a large
oiled bowl and cover
dough with plastic wrap.
Allow to stand in a warm
place for 1 hour or until
doubled in size.
3 Grease and line an 8in
(20cm) round cake pan.
Punch down dough with a
fist, then turn out onto a
lightly floured work surface.
Knead until smooth, then
roll into a 10in x 16in
(25cm x 42cm) rectangle.
Spread extra butter over
dough; scatter with dried

cranberries and sprinkle
with combined remaining
cinnamon, allspice,
nutmeg, and brown sugar.
Roll up dough firmly from
a long side and trim ends;
cut into nine equal slices.
Place eight scrolls, cut-
side up and touching the
edge of the pan, and one in
the center. Cover and allow
to stand in a warm place for
30 minutes or until risen.
4 Place the wire rack in the
inner pot, then place the
pan on top. Cover with the
air-fryer lid. Select **BAKE**
and set temperature to
325°F/160°C and time for
30 minutes; **BAKE** until
buns are golden brown.
5 Meanwhile, to make the
icing, sift powdered sugar
into a small bowl; stir in
enough of the extra milk to
form a thin, smooth paste.
6 Carefully remove pan
from the inner pot. Turn
buns out onto a wire rack
and drizzle with icing. Allow
to cool before serving.

MEATBALLS WITH MOZZARELLA & ORZO

Prep 10 mins   **Sauté** 10 mins   **Bake** 40 mins   **Serves** 4   Good to freeze

2 medium red onions, about 12oz
  (340g) in total
2 tbsp extra virgin olive oil
4 garlic cloves, crushed
2 x 14oz (411g) cans diced tomatoes
2 tbsp tomato purée
1½ cups (375ml) beef stock
1 tbsp light soft brown sugar
1 tbsp balsamic vinegar
1 cup (220g) orzo
⅓ cup (55g) pitted Sicilian
  green olives, torn

MEATBALLS
1oz (25g) fresh oregano
1 lb (450g) ground pork and veal
½ cup (50g) firm mozzarella, grated
½ cup (50g) finely grated
  Parmesan cheese
1 egg
1 cup (70g) stale breadcrumbs
1¼ tsp sea salt flakes

1 Coarsely grate half an onion. Thinly slice remaining onions; set aside.

2 To make the meatballs, chop oregano and combine with grated onion, the ground pork and veal, mozzarella, half of the Parmesan cheese, egg, breadcrumbs, and salt; season with freshly ground black pepper. Using your hands, combine mixture very well. Shape ¼-cups of the mixture into balls and place on a tray. Cover and refrigerate until needed.

3 Select **SAUTÉ** high heat and preheat for 8 minutes. When the inner pot is hot, add oil, then add the meatballs; **SAUTÉ**, turning, for 2 minutes or until meatballs are browned. Transfer meatballs to a tray to keep warm.

4 Add sliced onions to the inner pot and **SAUTÉ** for 5 minutes or until soft and golden. Add garlic and **SAUTÉ**, stirring for a further 1 minute or until fragrant. Add tomatoes, tomato purée, stock, sugar, and vinegar, then season well with salt and pepper; bring to a boil, then add the meatballs.

5 Cover with the air-fryer lid. Select **BAKE** and set temperature to 350°F/180°C and time for 30 minutes.

6 Add orzo and olives to the inner pot; stir gently to combine. Cover again with the air-fryer lid. Select **BAKE** and set temperature to 350°F/180°C and time for 10 minutes; **BAKE** until orzo is tender.

7 Serve meatballs and orzo sprinkled with remaining Parmesan cheese.

BANANA CAKE WITH CREAM CHEESE FROSTING & MISO CARAMEL

Prep 15 mins   **Bake** 1 hr 30 mins   **Sauté** 5 mins   **Serves** 8

11 tbsp (150g) unsalted butter, melted
½ cup (110g) firmly packed dark soft brown sugar
¼ cup (90g) honey
¼ cup (60g) white miso paste (shiro miso)
2 eggs
1 cup (280g) mashed ripe banana
2¼ cups (300g) flour
1½ tsp baking powder
1½ tsp baking soda
1 tsp salt
1½ tsp ground cinnamon
½ cup (55g) coarsely chopped walnuts
½ cup (125ml) buttermilk

MISO CARAMEL
1 cup (350g) honey
1 cup (250ml) whipping cream
1½ tbsp white miso paste (shiro miso)

CREAM CHEESE FROSTING
13oz (375g) cream cheese
½ cup (80g) powdered sugar

1 Grease a 7in (18cm) round cake pan; line the bottom and sides with parchment paper.

2 Whisk together butter, sugar, honey, miso paste, and eggs in a medium bowl until well combined; stir in banana. Fold in combined dry ingredients and cinnamon, walnuts, and buttermilk until well combined. Pour mixture into the pan and smooth the surface. Cover loosely with aluminum foil.

3 Place the air-fryer base in the inner pot, then place the pan on top. Cover with the air-fryer lid. Select **BAKE** and set temperature to 350°F/180°C and time for 1 hour 10 minutes.

4 Remove the aluminum foil, then cover again with the air-fryer lid. Select **BAKE** and set temperature to 350°F/180°C and time

for 20 minutes; **BAKE** until a skewer inserted in the center comes out clean.

5 Remove the pan from the inner pot. Allow the cake to cool in the pan for 10 minutes, before turning top-side up onto a wire rack to cool completely.

6 Meanwhile, to make the miso caramel, select **SAUTÉ** high heat. Add honey to the inner pot; **SAUTÉ** for 3 minutes or until darkened. Taking care, as mixture will splatter, stir in first cream, then miso, until smooth. Allow to cool to room temperature.

7 To make the cream cheese frosting, process ingredients until smooth. Refrigerate until needed.

8 Spread the top of the cake with cream cheese frosting, then drizzle with miso caramel.

HAM HOCK, CHICKEN & LEEK PIE

Prep 15 mins   **Sauté** 16 mins   **Bake** 20 mins   **Serves** 4   Good to freeze

1¾ lb (800g) boneless, skinless chicken thighs, trimmed and thinly sliced

2 tbsp extra virgin olive oil

1 large leek, about 1lb 2oz (500g), thinly sliced

2 garlic cloves, crushed

1 tbsp thyme leaves

¼ cup (35g) flour

3 cups (750ml) chicken stock

1¼ lb (600g) ham hock, meat removed, shredded

2 sheets of puff pastry, thawed

1 egg, lightly beaten

to serve: extra thyme sprigs

1 Select **SAUTÉ** high heat and preheat for 5 minutes. Season chicken with salt and pepper. When the inner pot is hot, add half of the oil, then add half of the chicken; **SAUTÉ**, stirring occasionally, for 3 minutes or until browned. Transfer chicken to a plate. Repeat with remaining oil and chicken; transfer to plate.

2 Add leek to the inner pot and **SAUTÉ**, stirring occasionally, for 3 minutes or until softened. Add garlic and thyme; **SAUTÉ** for a further 1 minute or until fragrant. Return chicken to the inner pot and add the flour; **SAUTÉ**, stirring, for 1 minute. Gradually stir in stock and bring to a boil; **SAUTÉ**, stirring continuously, for a further 5 minutes or until slightly thickened. Stir in ham and season with salt and pepper to taste. Check

a deep 8in (20cm) pie pan or baking dish fits in the inner pot, then transfer filling to the pan. Wipe the inner pot clean and return to the appliance. Place the wire rack in the pot.

3 Trim pastry to fit the top of the pan, then brush with egg. Place the pan on the wire rack in the inner pot. Cover with the air-fryer lid. Select **BAKE** and set temperature to 400°F/200°C and time for 20 minutes; **BAKE** until pastry is golden.

4 Serve pie scattered with extra thyme sprigs.

TIP The pie filling can be made up to 2 days ahead; cover and keep refrigerated until needed. The baked pie can be frozen for up to 3 months.

NO-KNEAD UKRAINIAN DINNER ROLLS (PAMPUSHKY)

Prep 15 mins (+ standing)   **Bake** 1 hr   **Serves** 8   Good to freeze   Vegetarian

2¼ tsp (7g) or 1 packet dried yeast
¼ cup (55g) sugar
½ cup (125ml) warm water
4⅔ cups (600g) bread flour, plus
   extra for dusting
2 tsp fine sea salt
2 eggs, lightly beaten
7 tbsp (90g) butter, melted
about ¾ cup (180ml) milk
1 egg yolk, beaten with 2 tsp water
1 garlic clove, crushed
¼ cup (7g) coarsely chopped
   flat-leaf parsley

TIP You can also use the appliance to proof the dough in steps 2 and 3. To do this, place a folded kitchen towel in the bottom of the inner pot, then place the bowl/cake pan on top. Select **WARM** and set for the specified time.

1 Whisk together yeast, 1 tablespoon of the sugar, and the water in a medium bowl until dissolved. Allow to stand for 10 minutes or until mixture is frothy.

2 Put flour, salt, and remaining sugar in a large bowl; make a well in the center. Pour in yeast mixture, beaten eggs, and 4 tablespoons of melted butter; stir in enough milk to form a soft, sticky dough. Cover with a damp kitchen towel. Allow to stand in a warm place for 45 minutes or until doubled in size.

3 Punch down dough with a fist; turn out onto a lightly floured work surface. Fold over several times until smooth. Divide into eight equal portions, then roll into balls. Grease an 8in (22cm) round cake pan. Place seven dough balls around the edge of the pan and one in the center. Cover with a damp kitchen

towel. Allow to stand in a warm place for 20 minutes or until doubled in size.

4 Place air-fryer basket in the inner pot. Cover with air-fryer lid. Select **BAKE** and set temperature to 400°F/200°C and time for 8 minutes to preheat.

5 Brush rolls with egg yolk wash. Place pan in the inner pot. Cover with the air-fryer lid. Select **BAKE** and set temperature to 350°F/180°C and time for 10 minutes.

6 Cover rolls with foil, then with the air-fryer lid. Select **BAKE** and set temperature to 350°F/180°C and time for 50 minutes; **BAKE** until rolls sound hollow when tapped. Leave in the pan for 5 minutes before transferring to a wire rack.

7 Combine garlic, parsley, and remaining butter in a small bowl. Brush warm rolls with the garlic butter and serve warm.

MEXICAN MAC & CHEESE

Prep 10 mins   **Sauté** 7 mins   **Bake** 15 mins   **Serves** 4   Good to freeze   Vegetarian

1 lb (450g) elbow macaroni
4 tbsp (60g) butter, chopped
½ cup (60g) flour
3 cups (750ml) milk
¼ cup (65g) chipotle in adobo
  sauce, chopped
8oz (225g) Mexican shredded cheese
2 ears corn on the cob, about
  1 lb 2oz (500g) in total,
  husks and silk removed
3 spring onions (scallions),
  thinly sliced
1 cup (100g) corn chips, crushed
to serve: hot sauce and chopped
  cilantro leaves

1 Bring a saucepan of salted water to a boil. Cook pasta for 2 minutes, then drain well. (The macaroni will be only partially cooked at this stage.)

2 Meanwhile, select **SAUTÉ** high heat and preheat for 5 minutes. When the inner pot is hot, add butter. Once butter is melted, add flour; **SAUTÉ**, stirring, for 1 minute or until a sandy texture. Gradually add milk, stirring for 3 minutes until smooth and well combined. Add chipotle and half of the cheese; **SAUTÉ**, stirring, for 2 minutes until cheese is melted. Stir in half of the spring onions and all of the macaroni; season with salt and freshly ground black pepper. Scatter with remaining cheese.

3 Cover with the air-fryer lid. Select **BAKE** and set temperature to 350°F/180°C and time for 15 minutes; **BAKE** until the top is golden.

4 Serve mac and cheese topped with corn chips, hot sauce, cilantro leaves, and spring onions.

PINK GRAPEFRUIT & POPPY SEED POUND CAKE

Prep 15 mins   **Dehydrate** 4 hrs   **Bake** 1 hr 35 mins   **Serves** 6–8

3 ruby red grapefruit, about 1½lb
    (700g) in total
1 cup (250g) butter, softened
1 cup (220g) sugar
1½ tbsp poppy seeds
4 eggs
1¾ cups (225g) flour
1½ tsp baking powder
1 tsp baking soda
1 tsp salt
1¾ cups (280g) powdered sugar

1 Thinly slice one of the grapefruit. Place the air-fryer basket in the inner pot. Arrange half of the grapefruit slices over the bottom of the basket, then place the perforated tray on top. Place remaining slices on the tray. Cover with the air-fryer lid. Select **DEHYDRATE** and set temperature to 155°F/70°C and time for 4 hours. Transfer grapefruit slices to a plate to cool.

2 Grease a deep 7in (18cm) round cake pan; line the bottom with parchment paper. Cover with the air-fryer lid. Select **BAKE** and set temperature to 350°F/180°C and time for 10 minutes to preheat.

3 Finely grate the zest from remaining grapefruit, then juice; you will need 2 tablespoons zest and ¼ cup (60ml) juice. Beat butter, sugar, grapefruit zest, and poppy seeds in a large bowl with an electric mixer until light and fluffy. Beat in eggs one at a time. Fold in dry ingredients in two batches. Spread mixture in pan and cover tightly with aluminum foil.

4 Place the air-fryer base in the inner pot, then place the pan on top. Cover with the air-fryer lid. Select **BAKE** and set temperature to 350°F/180°C and time for 1 hour 15 minutes.

5 Remove aluminum foil, then cover again with the air-fryer lid. Select **BAKE** and set temperature to 350°F/180°C and time for 20 minutes; **BAKE** until a skewer inserted in the center comes out clean. Remove pan from the inner pot. Leave cake in the pan for 10 minutes, then turn out, top-side up, onto a wire rack to cool completely.

6 Whisk powdered sugar and juice in a small bowl until smooth. Spread over cake; top with dehydrated grapefruit slices.

CONVERSION CHART

MEASURES

One Australian metric measuring cup holds approximately 250ml; one Australian metric tablespoon holds 20ml; one Australian metric teaspoon holds 5ml. North America, New Zealand, and the United Kingdom use a 15ml tablespoon. The difference between one country's measuring cups and another's is within a two- or three-teaspoon variance and will not affect cooking results. All cup and spoon measurements are level. The most accurate way of measuring dry ingredients is to weigh them. When measuring liquids, use a clear glass or plastic jug with metric markings.

We use large to extra-large eggs with an average weight of 2oz (60g) each.

DRY MEASURES

metric	imperial
15g	½oz
30g	1oz
60g	2oz
90g	3oz
125g	4oz (¼lb)
155g	5oz
185g	6oz
220g	7oz
250g	8oz (½lb)
280g	9oz
315g	10oz
345g	11oz
375g	12oz (¾lb)
410g	13oz
440g	14oz
470g	15oz
500g	16oz (1lb)
750g	24oz (1½lb)
1kg	32oz (2lb)

LIQUID MEASURES

metric	imperial
30ml	1 fluid oz
60ml	2 fluid oz
100ml	3 fluid oz
125ml	4 fluid oz
150ml	5 fluid oz
190ml	6 fluid oz
250ml	8 fluid oz
300ml	10 fluid oz
500ml	16 fluid oz
600ml	20 fluid oz
1000ml (1 liter)	1¾ pints

LENGTH MEASURES

metric	imperial
3mm	⅛in
6mm	¼in
1cm	½in
2cm	¾in
2.5cm	1in
5cm	2in
6cm	2½in
8cm	3in
10cm	4in
13cm	5in
15cm	6in
18cm	7in
20cm	8in
22cm	9in
25cm	10in
28cm	11in
30cm	12in (1ft)

OVEN TEMPERATURES

The oven temperatures below are for conventional ovens; if you are using a fan-forced oven, reduce the temperature by 20 degrees.

	°C (Celsius)	°F (Fahrenheit)
Very slow	120	250
Slow	150	300
Moderately slow	160	325
Moderate	180	350
Moderately hot	200	400
Hot	220	425
Very hot	240	475

Measurements for cake pans are approximate only. Using same-shaped cake pans of a similar size should not affect the outcome of your baking. We measure the inside top of the cake pan to determine size.

INDEX

Project Editor Siobhán O'Connor
DTP and Design Coordinator Heather Blagden
Jacket Designer Maxine Pedliham
Assistant Editor Jasmin Lennie
US Editors Sharon Lucas, Renee Wilmeth, Lori Hand
Jacket Coordinator Abi Gain
Senior Production Editor Tony Phipps
Senior Production Controller Stephanie McConnell
Editorial Director Cara Armstrong
Art Director Maxine Pedliham
Publishing Director Katie Cowan

DK DELHI
Managing Art Editor Neha Ahuja
DTP Coordinator Pushpak Tyagi
DTP Designer Satish Gaur
Pre-production Manager Balwant Singh

First American Edition, 2023
Published in the United States by DK Publishing
1745 Broadway, 20th Floor, New York, NY 10019

For the curious
www.dk.com